WORKING PAPERS
CHAPTERS 1-6
to accompany

ACCOUNTING PRINCIPLES
5th Edition

JERRY J. WEYGANDT Ph.D., C.P.A.
Arthur Andersen Alumni Professor of Accounting
University of Wisconsin - Madison
Madison, Wisconsin

DONALD E. KIESO Ph.D., C.P.A.
KPMG Peat Marwick Emeritus Professor of Accounting
Northern Illinois University
DeKalb, Illinois

PAUL D. KIMMEL Ph.D., C.P.A.
Associate Professor of Accounting
University of Wisconsin - Milwaukee
Milwaukee, Wisconsin

Prepared By
ANNE LEE BAIN M.A., C.P.A.
Assistant Professor of Accounting
St. Cloud State University
St. Cloud, Minnesota

JOHN WILEY & SONS, INC.
New York • Chichester • Weinheim • Brisbane • Singapore • Toronto

COVER PHOTO © Paul Souders/Tony Stone Images, New York

ISBN 0-471-24895-9

Printed in the United States of America

10 9 8 7 6 5 4 3 2 1

Printed and bound by Courier Kendallville, Inc.

NOTE TO THE STUDENT

These working papers contain solution forms for all Brief Exercises, Exercises, and Problems in Weygandt et al., *Accounting Principles*, 5th edn., chapters 1–6. From the "Broadening Your Perspective" section at the end of each chapter, the working papers also contain solution forms for each Financial Reporting Problem, Comparative Analysis Problem, Financial Statement Interpretation, Real-World Focus, Group Decision Case, and Ethics Case. Because the solutions to the remaining "Broadening Your Perspective" problems tend to be free-form, there are no working papers for any of the problems entitled "Research Assignment," "Communication Activity," or "Surfing the Net." There are, likewise, no working paper solution forms for any of the Self-Study Questions or chapter Questions at the end of each chapter.

In general, the working papers follow the organization of the textbook. To maximize the use of space, however, forms for the Exercises occasionally appear out of order and the Real-World Focus and Ethics Case solution forms frequently appear on the same page at the end of each chapter's working papers. And several problems for Chapter 4 (P4- 1A, P4-4A, P4-5A, P4-6A, P4-1B, P4-4B, and P4-5B), Chapter 5 (P5-3A and P5-3B), and the Chapter 6 Financial Reporting Problem (Mini-Practice Set) require 11" x 17" sheets, which are separately bound in the back of this volume.

Name

Section

Date

Name

Section

Date

Name

Section

Date

#1

#2

#3

Name

Section

Date

Exercise 1-4

Maria Mendoza & Co.

(a)

(b)

(c)

Name **Exercise 1-5**

Section

Date **Maria Mendoza & Co.**

Name

Section

Date

Exercise 1-6

Dylan Company

(a)

(b)

(c)

Name

Section

Date

Exercise 1-7

Anne Wyatt, D.D.S., & Rambo Enterprises

(a)

(b)

(c)

(d)

Name

Section

Date

Exercise 1-8

Dyna Jeng Co.

Name

Section

Date

#9

#10

Bear Park
Balance Sheet
December 31, 1999
Assets

Cash			20000
Cash		$	20000
Equipment	115,500		140000
Supplies			2500
	137500		162500

Liabilities and Owners Equity

Liabilities			
Accounts payable		$	11000
Notes payable	71,000		60000
Owners Equity			69500
Total Liabilities + owner's equity			140500

Name

Section

Date

Exercises 1-11 to 1-12

#11

#12

Name **Problem 1-1A**

Section

Date **Wayne State Travel Agency**

(a)

WAYNE STATE TRAVEL AGENCY

	Assets							=	Liabilities	+	Owner's Equity
Trans-actions	Cash	+	Accounts Receivable	+	Supplies	+	Office Equip-ment	=	Accounts Payable	+	Merle Peper Capital
1.											
2.											
3.											
4.											
5.											
6.											
7.											
8.											
9.											
10.											

Name

Section

Date

Problem 1-1A Concluded

Wayne State Travel Agency

(b)

Name

Section

Date

Problem 1-2A

George Kanaan, Attorney at Law

(a)

GEORGE KANAAN, ATTORNEY AT LAW

Trans-action	Assets: Cash	+ Accounts Receivable	+ Supplies	+ Office Equipment	= Liabilities: Notes Payable	+ Accounts Payable	+ Owner's Equity: George Kanaan, Capital	
Bal.	$4,000	$1,500	$500	$5,000		$4,200	$6,800	
1.	+ 1,400	− (1,400)						
	5,400	$2,100	$500	$5,000 =		$4,200	$6,800	
2.	− 2,700					− 2,700		
	$2,700	2,100	500	5,000		$1,500	6,800	
3.	$3,000	+$3,400					+$6,400	
	$5,700	3,500	500	5,000		$1,500	$13,200	
4.	− (400)			+ 1,000		+ 600		
	$5,300	3,500	500	6,000		$2,100	$13,200	
5.	− 3,750						− 2,500	Salaries
							− 900	Rent
							− 350	Advertising
6.	$1,550	3,500	500	6,000		$2,100	$9,450	
	− (550)						(550)	
	1,000	3,500	500	6,000		$2,100	8,900	
7.	+ 2,000					+ 2,000		
	3,000	3,500	500	6,000		$4,100	$8,900	
8.						(250)	(250)	
	3,000	3,500	500	6,000		3,850	8,650	

8650

Name

Section

Date

Problem 1-2A Continued

George Kanaan, Attorney at Law

(b)

GEORGE KANAAN, ATTORNEY AT LAW

Income Statement

For the Month Ended August 31, 1999

Revenues	
Expenses	
Net Income (loss)	

GEORGE KANAAN, ATTORNEY AT LAW

Owner's Equity Statement

For the Month Ended August 31, 1999

Name

Section

Date

(b) (Continued)

GEORGE KANAAN, ATTORNEY AT LAW
Balance Sheet
August 31, 1999

Assets

Liabilities and Owner's Equity

Name | **Problem 1-3A**

Section

Date | **Secret Cosmetics Co.**

(a)

SECRET COSMETICS CO.
Income Statement
For the Month Ended June 30, 1999

Revenues

Expenses

Net Income (loss)

SECRET COSMETICS CO.
Owner's Equity Statement
For the Month Ended June 30, 1999

(a) (Continued)

SECRET COSMETICS CO.
Balance Sheet
June 30, 1999

Assets		
Liabilities and Owner's Equity		

(b)

SECRET COSMETICS CO.
Income Statement
For the Month Ended June 30, 1999

Revenues		
Expenses		
Net Income (loss)		

(b) (Continued)

SECRET COSMETICS CO.
Owner's Equity Statement
For the Month Ended June 30, 1999

Name

Section

Date

Problem 1-4A

Bell Consulting

(a)

BELL CONSULTING

Date	Assets				=	Liabilities		+	Owner' Equity	
	Cash	+ Accounts Receivable	+ Supplies	+ Office Equipment	=	Notes Payable	+ Accounts Payable		+ J. Bell, Capital	Explanation
May 1										
2										
3										
5										
9										
12										
15										
17										
20										
23										
26										
29										
30										

(b)

BELL CONSULTING

Income Statement

For the Month Ended May 31, 1999

Revenues

Expenses

Net income

(c)

BELL CONSULTING

Balance Statement

May 31, 1999

Assets

Liabilities and Owner's Equity

Name

Section

Date

Problem 1-5A

Montreal Company and Others

(a)

	Montreal Company	Calgary Company	Edmonton Company	Vancouver Company

(b) and (c)

(b)

MONTREAL COMPANY

Owner's Equity Statement

For the Year Ended December 31, 1999

(c)

Name **Problem 1-1B**

Section

Date **Kumar's Repair Shop**

(a)

KUMAR'S REPAIR SHOP

Assets = Liabilities + Owner's Equity

Transactions	Cash	+ Accounts Receivable	+ Supplies	+ Equipment	= Accounts Payable	+ U. Kumar, Capital
1.						
2.						
3.						
4.						
5.						
6.						
7.						
8.						
9.						
10.						
11.						

Name

Section

Date

Kumar's Repair Shop

(b)

Name

Section

Date

Problem 1-2B

Bruce Smith, Veterinarian

(a)

BRUCE SMITH, VETERINARIAN

	Assets							=	Liabilities			+	Owner's Equity
Trans-actions	Cash	+	Accounts Receivable	+	Supplies	+	Office Equipment	=	Notes Payable	+	Accounts Payable	+	Bruce Smith, Capital
Bal.	$9,000	+	$1,700	+	$600	+	$6,000	=		+	$3,600	+	$13,700
1.													
2.													
3.													
4.													
5.													
6.													
7.													
8.													

(b)

BRUCE SMITH, VETERINARIAN
Income Statement
For the Month Ended September 30, 1999

Revenues

Expenses

Net Income (loss)

BRUCE SMITH, VETERINARIAN
Owner's Equity Statement
For the Month Ended September 30, 1999

(b) (Continued)

BRUCE SMITH, VETERINARIAN
Balance Sheet
September 30, 1999

Assets		
Liabilities and Owner's Equity		

Name **Problem 1-3B**

Section

Date **Ruston Flying School**

(a)

RUSTON FLYING SCHOOL

Income Statement

For the Month Ended May 31, 1999

Revenues	
Expenses	
Net Income (loss)	

RUSTON FLYING SCHOOL

Owner's Equity Statement

For the Month Ended May 31, 1999

(a) (Continued)

RUSTON FLYING SCHOOL
Balance Sheet
May 31, 1999

Assets

Liabilities and Owner's Equity

(b)

RUSTON FLYING SCHOOL
Income Statement
For the Month Ended May 31, 1999

Revenues

Expenses

Net Income (loss)

(b) (Continued)

RUSTON FLYING SCHOOL
Owner's Equity Statement
For the Month Ended May 31, 1999

Name

Section

Date

Problem 1-4B

Alex Deliveries

(a)

ALEX DELIVERIES

Date	Assets				=	Liabilities		+	Owner' Equity	
	Cash	+ Accounts Receivable	+ Supplies	+ Delivery Van	=	Notes Payable	+ Accounts Payable	+	P. Alex, Capital	Explanation
May 1										
2										
3										
5										
9										
12										
15										
17										
20										
23										
26										
29										
30										

(b)

ALEX DELIVERIES Income Statement For the Month Ended June 30, 1999		
Revenues		
Expenses		
Net income		

(c)

ALEX DELIVERIES Balance Statement June 30, 1999		
Assets		
Liabilities and Owner's Equity		

Name

Section

Date

Problem 1-5B

Marshall Company and Others

(a)

	Loyola Company	Marshall Company	UNLV Company	UNC Company

(b) and (c)

(b)

MARSHALL COMPANY

Owner's Equity Statement

For the Year Ended December 31, 1999

(c)

Name

Section

Date

Kellogg Company

(a)

(b)

(c)

(d) Net sales—1995 (in thousands)

1996 (in thousands)

1997 (in thousands)

(e)

Name

Section

Date

Chapter 1 Comparative Analysis Problem

Kellogg vs. General Mills

(a) (In millions)	General Mills	Kellogg
1. Total assets		
2. Accounts receivable		
3. Net sales		
4. Net income		

(b)

Assets

Cash

Accounts receivable

Machinery and Equipment, net

Other noncurrent assets

Total assets

Calculations

(a) Cash

(b) Accounts receivable

(c) Machinery and Equipment, net

(d) Other noncurrent assets

(a)

(b)

LONG-SHOT DRIVING RANGE
Balance Sheet
March 31,1999

Assets

Liabilities and Owner's Equity

Name
Section
Date

(c) and (d)

(c)

(d)

REAL-WORLD FOCUS Air Transportation Holding Company

(a)

(b)

(c)

ETHICS CASE Steve Pelli, Job Interviewee

(a)

(b)

(c)

Name

Section

Date

Name

Section

Date

Name

Section

Date

General Journal

Date	Account Titles and Explanation	Ref.	Debit	Credit

Date	Explanation	Ref.	Debit	Credit	Balance

Date	Explanation	Ref.	Debit	Credit	Balance

Date	Explanation	Ref.	Debit	Credit	Balance

Name

Section

Date

Name

Section

Date

Exercise 2-1

L. Visser, Interior Decorator

Transaction Date	Account Debited (a) Basic Type	(b) Specific Account	(c) Effect	(d) Normal Balance	Account Credited (a) Basic Type	(b) Specific Account	(c) Effect	(d) Normal Balance
Jan.								
2	Asset	Cash	Increase	Debit	Owner's	L. Visser,	Increase	Credit
					Equity	Capital		
3								
9								
11								
16								
20								
23								
28								

Name **Exercise 2-2**

Section

Date **L. Visser, Interior Decorator**

General Journal

	Date	Account Titles and Explanation	Ref.	Debit	Credit	
1						1
2						2
3						3
4						4
5						5
6						6
7						7
8						8
9						9
10						10
11						11
12						12
13						13
14						14
15						15
16						16
17						17
18						18
19						19
20						20
21						21
22						22
23						23
24						24
25						25
26						26
27						27
28						28
29						29
30						30
31						31
32						32
33						33
34						34
35						35
36						36
37						37
38						38
39						39
40						40

Name

Section

Date

Exercises 2-3 to 2-4

Stine Real Estate Agency

#3

#4

Date	Account Titles and Explanation	Ref.	Debit	Credit

Name

Section

Date

Exercise 2-5

J. L. Meche, Investment Broker

(a)

CASH	

NOTES PAYABLE	

ACCOUNTS RECEIVABLE	

J. L. MECHE, CAPITAL	

OFFICE EQUIPMENT	

SERVICE REVENUE	

(b)

J. L. MECHE, INVESTMENT BROKER
Trial Balance
August 31, 1999

	Debit	Credit

Name

Section

Date

Exercise 2-6

Doty Landscaping Company

(a)

General Journal

Date	Account Titles and Explanation	Ref.	Debit	Credit

(b)

DOTY LANDSCAPING COMPANY
Trial Balance
April 30, 1999

	Debit	Credit

Name

Section

Date

Exercise 2-7

McBride Co.

(a) General Journal

Date	Account Titles and Explanation	Ref.	Debit	Credit

(b)

McBRIDE CO.
Trial Balance
October 31, 1999

	Debit	Credit

Name | **Exercise 2-8**

Section

Date | **Tracy Lawrence Company**

(a) General Journal J1

	Date	Account Titles and Explanation	Ref.	Debit	Credit	
1						1
2						2
3						3
4						4
5						5
6						6
7						7
8						8
9						9
10						10
11						11
12						12

(b) Cash No. 101

Date	Explanation	Ref.	Debit	Credit	Balance

Equipment No. 157

Date	Explanation	Ref.	Debit	Credit	Balance

Accounts Payable No. 201

Date	Explanation	Ref.	Debit	Credit	Balance

Tracy Lawrence, Capital No. 301

Date	Explanation	Ref.	Debit	Credit	Balance

Tracy Lawrence, Drawing No. 306

Date	Explanation	Ref.	Debit	Credit	Balance

Name

Section

Date

#9

Error	(a) In Balance?	(b) Difference	(c) Larger Column
1. Credit posting of $400 to Accounts	No	$400	Debit
Receivable was omitted			
2.			
3.			
4.			
5.			
6.			

#10

ALWAYS LATE DELIVERY SERVICE
Trial Balance
July 31, 1999

	Debit	Credit

Name | **Problem 2-1A**

Section

Date | **Four Oaks Miniature Golf and Driving Range**

General Journal | J1

Date	Account Titles and Explanation	Ref.	Debit	Credit

Name | **Problem 2-1A Concluded**

Section

Date | **Four Oaks Miniature Golf and Driving Range**

General Journal J2

Date	Account Titles and Explanation	Ref.	Debit	Credit

Name | **Problem 2-2A**

Section

Date | **Maria Rojas, Architect**

(a) General Journal J1

Date	Account Titles and Explanation	Ref.	Debit	Credit
1999				
April 1	Cash	101	15000	
	Maria Rojas Capital	301		15000
	(owners investment of cash in bus.)			
2	Rent Expense	729	1800	
	Cash	101		1800
	(office rent for the month)			
3	Architectural supplies	126	1500	
	Accounts payable	201		1500
	(purchased supplies on Account)			
10	Accounts Receivable	112	900	
	Service Revenue	400		900
	(billed client for complete blueprints)			
11	~~Unearned Revenue~~ Cash	205	500	
	~~Maria Rojas Capital~~	301		500
	(Unearned Revenue			
20	Cash	101	1500	
	Service Revenue	400		1500
30	Salary Expense		1200	
	Cash	101		1200

Name
Section
Date

Problem 2-2A Continued

Maria Rojas, Architect

(b)

Cash — No. 101

Date	Explanation	Ref.	Debit	Credit	Balance
		J1	15000		
		J1	800		
		J1	500		14700
			1500		16200
					15000
				600	14400

Accounts Receivable — No. 112

Date	Explanation	Ref.	Debit	Credit	Balance

Supplies — No. 126

Date	Explanation	Ref.	Debit	Credit	Balance

Accounts Payable — No. 201

Date	Explanation	Ref.	Debit	Credit	Balance

Revenue — No. 205

Date	Explanation	Ref.	Debit	Credit	Balance

Maria Rojas, Capital — No. 301

Date	Explanation	Ref.	Debit	Credit	Balance

(b) (Continued)

Service Revenue No. 400

Date	Explanation	Ref.	Debit	Credit	Balance

Salaries Expense No. 726

Date	Explanation	Ref.	Debit	Credit	Balance

Rent Expense No. 729

Date	Explanation	Ref.	Debit	Credit	Balance

(c)

MARIA ROJAS, ARCHITECT
Trial Balance
April 30, 1999

		Debit	Credit	
1	Cash	14400		1
2	Accounts Receivable	900		2
3	Supplies	1500		3
4	Accounts Payable		900	4
5	Unearned Revenue		500	5
6	Maria Rojas, Capital		15000	6
7	Service Revenue		2400	7
8	Salaries Expense		1200	8
9	Rent Expense	800		9
10				10
11				11

Name **Problem 2-3A**

Section

Date **Judy's Laundry**

(a) and (c)

Cash — No. 101

Date	Explanation	Ref.	Debit	Credit	Balance

Accounts Receivable — No. 112

Date	Explanation	Ref.	Debit	Credit	Balance

Supplies — No. 126

Date	Explanation	Ref.	Debit	Credit	Balance

Equipment — No. 157

Date	Explanation	Ref.	Debit	Credit	Balance

Accounts Payable — No. 201

Date	Explanation	Ref.	Debit	Credit	Balance

Unearned Revenue — No. 206

Date	Explanation	Ref.	Debit	Credit	Balance

(a) and (c) (Continued)

Judy Kylie, Capital — No. 301

Date	Explanation	Ref.	Debit	Credit	Balance

Judy Kylie, Drawing — No. 306

Date	Explanation	Ref.	Debit	Credit	Balance

Laundry Revenue — No. 426

Date	Explanation	Ref.	Debit	Credit	Balance

Salaries Expense — No. 726

Date	Explanation	Ref.	Debit	Credit	Balance

Utilities Expense — No. 732

Date	Explanation	Ref.	Debit	Credit	Balance

(d)

JUDY'S LAUNDRY
Trial Balance
October 31, 1999

		Debit	Credit	
1	Cash			1
2	Accounts Receivable			2
3	Supplies			3
4	Equipment			4
5	Accounts Payable			5
6	Unearned Revenue			6
7	Judy Kylie, Capital			7
8	Judy Kylie, Drawing			8
9	Laundry Revenue			9
10	Salaries Expense			10
11	Utilities Expense			11
12				12
13				13

Name

Section

Date

Judy's Laundry

(b) General Journal J1

Date	Account Titles and Explanation	Ref.	Debit	Credit

Name | **Problem 2-4A**

Section

Date | **Tim Winan Co.**

TIM WINAN CO.
Trial Balance
June 30, 1999

	Debit	Credit

Journal Entry Aids:

Name **Problem 2-5A**

Section

Date **Starlite Theater**

(a) and (c)

Cash No. 101

Date	Explanation	Ref.	Debit	Credit	Balance

Accounts Receivable No. 112

Date	Explanation	Ref.	Debit	Credit	Balance

Land No. 140

Date	Explanation	Ref.	Debit	Credit	Balance

Buildings No. 145

Date	Explanation	Ref.	Debit	Credit	Balance

Equipment No. 157

Date	Explanation	Ref.	Debit	Credit	Balance

Accounts Payable No. 201

Date	Explanation	Ref.	Debit	Credit	Balance

(a) and (c) (Continued)

L. Baroni, Capital No. 301

Date	Explanation	Ref.	Debit	Credit	Balance

Admission Revenue No. 405

Date	Explanation	Ref.	Debit	Credit	Balance

Concession Revenue No. 406

Date	Explanation	Ref.	Debit	Credit	Balance

Advertising Expense No. 610

Date	Explanation	Ref.	Debit	Credit	Balance

Film Rental Expense No. 632

Date	Explanation	Ref.	Debit	Credit	Balance

Salaries Expense No. 726

Date	Explanation	Ref.	Debit	Credit	Balance

Name | **Problem 2-5A Continued**

Section

Date | **Starlite Theater**

(b) General Journal J1

	Date	Account Titles and Explanation	Ref.	Debit	Credit	
1						1
2						2
3						3
4						4
5						5
6						6
7						7
8						8
9						9
10						10
11						11
12						12
13						13
14						14
15						15
16						16
17						17
18						18
19						19
20						20
21						21
22						22
23						23
24						24
25						25
26						26
27						27
28						28
29						29
30						30
31						31
32						32
33						33
34						34
35						35
36						36
37						37
38						38
39						39
40						40

(b) (Continued) General Journal J1

	Date	Account Titles and Explanation	Ref.	Debit	Credit	
1						1
2						2
3						3
4						4
5						5
6						6
7						7
8						8
9						9
10						10
11						11
12						12
13						13
14						14
15						15
16						16

(d)

STARLITE THEATER
Trial Balance
March 31, 1999

		Debit	Credit	
1	Cash			1
2	Accounts Receivable			2
3	Land			3
4	Equipment			4
5	Accounts Payable			5
6	L. Baroni, Capital			6
7	Admission Revenue			7
8	Concession Revenue			8
9	Advertising Expense			9
10	Film Rental Expense			10
11	Salaries Expense			11
12				12
13				13
14				14
15				15

Name **Problem 2-1B**

Section

Date **Adventure Park**

General Journal J1

Date	Account Titles and Explanation	Ref.	Debit	Credit

Name **Problem 2-2B**

Section

Date **Lisa Heins, CPA**

(a) General Journal J1

Date	Account Titles and Explanation	Ref.	Debit	Credit

(b)

Cash No. 101

Date	Explanation	Ref.	Debit	Credit	Balance

Accounts Receivable No. 112

Date	Explanation	Ref.	Debit	Credit	Balance

Supplies No. 126

Date	Explanation	Ref.	Debit	Credit	Balance

Accounts Payable No. 201

Date	Explanation	Ref.	Debit	Credit	Balance

Unearned Revenue No. 205

Date	Explanation	Ref.	Debit	Credit	Balance

Lisa Heins, Capital No. 301

Date	Explanation	Ref.	Debit	Credit	Balance

(b) (Continued)

Service Revenue No. 400

Date	Explanation	Ref.	Debit	Credit	Balance

Salaries Expense No. 726

Date	Explanation	Ref.	Debit	Credit	Balance

Rent Expense No. 729

Date	Explanation	Ref.	Debit	Credit	Balance

(c)

LISA HEINS, CPA
Trial Balance
April 30, 1999

		Debit	Credit	
1	Cash			1
2	Accounts Receivable			2
3	Supplies			3
4	Accounts Payable			4
5	Unearned Revenue			5
6	Lisa Heins, Capital			6
7	Service Revenue			7
8	Salaries Expense			8
9	Rent Expense			9
10				10
11				11

Name **Problem 2-3B**

Section

Date **Steiner Dry Cleaners**

(a) and (c)

Cash No. 101

Date	Explanation	Ref.	Debit	Credit	Balance

Accounts Receivable No. 112

Date	Explanation	Ref.	Debit	Credit	Balance

Supplies No. 126

Date	Explanation	Ref.	Debit	Credit	Balance

Equipment No. 157

Date	Explanation	Ref.	Debit	Credit	Balance

Accounts Payable No. 201

Date	Explanation	Ref.	Debit	Credit	Balance

(a) and (c) (Continued)

Unearned Revenue No. 206

Date	Explanation	Ref.	Debit	Credit	Balance

C. Steiner, Capital No. 301

Date	Explanation	Ref.	Debit	Credit	Balance

C. Steiner, Drawing No. 306

Date	Explanation	Ref.	Debit	Credit	Balance

Dry Cleaning Revenue No. 428

Date	Explanation	Ref.	Debit	Credit	Balance

Repair Expense No. 622

Date	Explanation	Ref.	Debit	Credit	Balance

Salaries Expense No. 726

Date	Explanation	Ref.	Debit	Credit	Balance

Utilities Expense No. 732

Date	Explanation	Ref.	Debit	Credit	Balance

Name **Problem 2-3B Continued**

Section

Date **Steiner Dry Cleaners**

(b) General Journal J1

Date	Account Titles and Explanation	Ref.	Debit	Credit

Name

Section

Date

Problem 2-3B Concluded

Steiner Dry Cleaners

(d)

STEINER DRY CLEANERS
Trial Balance
July 31, 1999

	Debit	Credit
Cash		
Accounts Receivable		
Supplies		
Equipment		
Accounts Payable		
Unearned Revenue		
C. Steiner, Capital		
C. Steiner, Drawing		
Dry Cleaning Revenue		
Salaries Expense		
Utilities Expense		
Repair Expense		

Name

Section

Date

Problem 2-4B

Shawnee Company

SHAWNEE COMPANY

Trial Balance

May 31, 1999

	Debit	Credit

Journal Entry Aids:

Name　　　　　　　　　　　　　　　　　　　　**Problem 2-5B**

Section

Date　　　　　　　　　　　　　　　　　　　　**Grand Theater**

(a) and (c)

Cash　No. 101

Date	Explanation	Ref.	Debit	Credit	Balance

Accounts Receivable　No. 112

Date	Explanation	Ref.	Debit	Credit	Balance

Prepaid Rentals　No. 136

Date	Explanation	Ref.	Debit	Credit	Balance

Land　No. 140

Date	Explanation	Ref.	Debit	Credit	Balance

Buildings　No. 145

Date	Explanation	Ref.	Debit	Credit	Balance

Equipment　No. 157

Date	Explanation	Ref.	Debit	Credit	Balance

Accounts Payable　No. 201

Date	Explanation	Ref.	Debit	Credit	Balance

Name

Section

Date

Problem 2-5B Continued

Grand Theater

(a) and (c) (Continued)

Mortgage Payable — No. 275

Date	Explanation	Ref.	Debit	Credit	Balance

Frances Hill, Capital — No. 301

Date	Explanation	Ref.	Debit	Credit	Balance

Admission Revenue — No. 405

Date	Explanation	Ref.	Debit	Credit	Balance

Concession Revenue — No. 406

Date	Explanation	Ref.	Debit	Credit	Balance

Advertising Expense — No. 610

Date	Explanation	Ref.	Debit	Credit	Balance

Film Rental Expense — No. 632

Date	Explanation	Ref.	Debit	Credit	Balance

Salaries Expense — No. 726

Date	Explanation	Ref.	Debit	Credit	Balance

Name

Section

Date

Problem 2-5B Continued

Grand Theater

(b) General Journal J1

Date	Account Titles and Explanation	Ref.	Debit	Credit

Name

Section

Date

Problem 2-5B Concluded

Grand Theater

(b) (Continued)

General Journal

J1

Date	Account Titles and Explanation	Ref.	Debit	Credit

(d)

GRAND THEATER
Trial Balance
April 30, 1999

	Debit	Credit
Cash		
Accounts Receivable		
Prepaid Rentals		
Land		
Buildings		
Equipment		
Accounts Payable		
Mortgage Payable		
Fran Holley, Capital		
Admission Revenue		
Concession Revenue		
Advertising Expense		
Film Rental Expense		
Salaries Expense		

Name

Section

Date

Kellogg Company

(a)

Account	Side of Account for Increase	Side of Account for Decrease	Normal Balance
Accounts Payable			
Accounts Receivable			
Property			
Notes Payable			
Interest Expense			
Inventories			

(b) and (c)

	Accounts	Effect
(b) When		
Accounts Receivable is decreased		
Accounts Payable is decreased		
Inventories are increased		
(c) When		
Interest Expense is increased		
OR		
Property is increased		
OR		

Name

Section

Date

(a) Kellogg

1.

2.

3.

4.

General Mills

1.

2.

3.

4.

(b)

Name

Section

Date

Bob Evans Farms, Inc.

(a)

(b)

(c)

Name

Section

Date

Chapter 2 Group Decision Case

Daniels Riding Academy

(a) General Journal

Date	Account Titles and Explanation	Ref.	Debit	Credit

Name
Section
Date

(b)

(c) and (d)

(c) Net income as reported	4500
(d) Cash as reported	12475

Name

Section

Date

REAL-WORLD FOCUS Automated Security Holdings

(a)

(b)

(c)

ETHICS CASE Staples Company

(a)

(b)

(c)

Name

Section

Date

Name

Section

Date

Name

Section

Date

Name
Section
Date

Name

Section

Date

#1

Adj.	(a) Type of Adjustment	(b) Account Relationship	(c) Accounts before Adjustment
1.			
2.			
3.			
4.			
5.			
6.			

#2 General Journal

Date	Account Titles and Explanation	Ref.	Debit	Credit
1999	Adjusting Entries			
March 31	Depreciation Expense		250	
	Accumulated Depreciation Equipment			250
	(To record monthly depreciation)			
	Unearned Rent Revenue		1100	
	Service Revenue			1100
	(to record revenue for services provided)			
	Interest Expense		500	
	Interest payable			500
	(to record interest on notes payable)			
	Supplies Expense		1850	
	Supplies			1850
	(To record supplies used)			
	Insurance Expense		300	
	Prepaid Insurance			300
	(to record insurance expired)			

General Journal

Date	Account Titles and Explanation	Debit	Credit
#3	Adjusting Entries		
1999	Accounts Receivable	750	
Jan 31	Service Revenue		750
	(to record revenue earned and not billed)		
	Utilities Expense	520	
	Utilities payable		520
	(to record unpaid utilities)		
	Depreciation Expense	400	
	accumulated depreciation		400
	(to record monthly depreciation)		
	Interest expense	500	
	Interest payable		500
	(to record interest on notes payable)		
	Insurance Expense	1000	
	prepaid insurance		1000
	(to record insurance expired)		
	Supplies Expense	1100	
	Supplies		1100
	(to record dental supplies used)		
#4			
1999	Adjusting Entries		
Oct 31	Advertising Supplies Expense	1100	
	Advertising supplies		1100
	(to record supplies used)		
	Insurance Expense	100	
	prepaid insurance		100
	(to record insurance expired)		
	Depreciation expense	50	
	accumulated depreciation		50
	(to record monthly depreciation)		
	Unearned Revenue	600	
	Service revenue		600
	(to record revenue received but unearned)		
	Accounts Receivable	300	
	Service Revenue		300
	(to record earned but not billed)		
	Interest expense	70	
	interest payable		70
	(to record accrued interest)		
	Salaries Expense	1500	
	Salaries payable		1500
	(to record unpaid salaries)		

Name
Section
Date

Lanier Company
Income Statement
for the Month ended July 31

#5

Revenues
Service Revenue

#6

Name

Section

Date

Exercises 3-7 to 3-8

General Journal

Date	Account Titles and Explanations	Debit	Credit
#7			
#8			

Name
Section
Date

Exercise 3-9

Lund Company

LUND COMPANY
Income Statement
For the Year Ended August 31, 1999

Revenues		
Service Revenue		$34600
Rent Revenue		11800
		46400
Expenses		
Salaries Expenses	$18100	
Rent Expense	15000	
Office Supplies Expense	1600	
Insurance Expense	1500	
Depreciation Expense	1200	
Total Expenses		$37400
Net Income		9000

LUND COMPANY
Owner's Equity Statement
For the Year Ended August 31, 1999

R. Lori, Capital, Aug. 1, 1998	$ -0-
Add: Investments	15600
Net Income	9000
R. Lori, Capital Aug. 31, 1999	$24600

LUND COMPANY
Balance Sheet
August 31, 1999

Assets		
Cash		$10400
Accounts Receivable		9400
Office Supplies		700
Prepaid Insurance		2500
Office equipment	$14,000	
Less: Accumulated Depreciation	4,800	$9200
Total Assets		$32200
Liabilities and Owners Equity		
Liabilities		
Accounts Payable		$5800
Unearned Rent Revenue		700
Salaries Payable		1100
Total Liabilities		$7600
Owner's Equity		
R. Lori, Capital		$15600
Total Liabilities and Owners Equity		$23200

Name

Section

Date

Exercise 3-10

Cash vs. Accrual

(a)

(b)

(c)

Name

Section

Date

***Exercise 3-11**

Harmony Company

(a)

CASH	

SERVICE REVENUE	

INSURANCE EXPENSE	

SUPPLIES EXPENSE	

(b)

PREPAID INSURANCE	

INSURANCE EXPENSE	

SUPPLIES	

SUPPLIES EXPENSE	

UNEARNED REVENUE	

SERVICE REVENUE	

(c)

Name

Section

Date

Problem 3-1A

Midwest Tours

(a) General Journal J2

Date	Account Titles and Explanation	Ref.	Debit	Credit
1999	Adjusting Entries			
June 30	Insurance Expense		650	
	Prepaid Insurance			650
	(To record Ins. Expired)			
30	Depreciation Expense		50	
	Acc. Depreciation Office equipment			50
	(To record monthly depreciation)			
30	Depreciation Expense		2000	
	Acc. Depreciation Buses			2000
	(To record monthly depreciation)			
30	Interest Expense		700	
	Interest payable			700
	(To record interest on notes payable)			
30	Unearned Revenue		6000	
	Tour Revenue			6000
	(To record revenue for services provided)			
30	Salaries Expense		1200	
	Salaries Payable			1200
	(To record accrued salaries)			
30	Accounts Receivable		1200	
	Tour Revenue			1200
	(To record revenue for services provided)			

Name | **Problem 3-1A Continued**

Section

Date | **Midwest Tours**

(b)

Cash

Date	Explanation	Ref.	Debit	Credit	Balance
1999					
June 30		J2	3000		3000

Accounts Receivable

Date	Explanation	Ref.	Debit	Credit	Balance
1999					
Jun 30	Adj Entry	J2	1,200		1200

Prepaid Insurance

Date	Explanation	Ref.	Debit	Credit	Balance
1999					
Jun 30	Adj entry	J2	7800		7150
	Adj			650	

Office Equipment

Date	Explanation	Ref.	Debit	Credit	Balance

Accumulated Depreciation — Office Equipment

Date	Explanation	Ref.	Debit	Credit	Balance

Buses

Date	Explanation	Ref.	Debit	Credit	Balance

Accumulated Depreciation — Buses

Date	Explanation	Ref.	Debit	Credit	Balance

(b) (Continued)

Salaries Payable

Date	Explanation	Ref.	Debit	Credit	Balance

Interest Payable

Date	Explanation	Ref.	Debit	Credit	Balance

Notes Payable

Date	Explanation	Ref.	Debit	Credit	Balance

Unearned Tour Revenue

Date	Explanation	Ref.	Debit	Credit	Balance

Alan Kinsley, Capital

Date	Explanation	Ref.	Debit	Credit	Balance

Tour Revenue

Date	Explanation	Ref.	Debit	Credit	Balance

Salaries Expense

Date	Explanation	Ref.	Debit	Credit	Balance

(b) (Continued)

Advertising Expense

Date	Explanation	Ref.	Debit	Credit	Balance

Gas and Oil Expense

Date	Explanation	Ref.	Debit	Credit	Balance

Insurance Expense

Date	Explanation	Ref.	Debit	Credit	Balance

Depreciation Expense — Office Equipment

Date	Explanation	Ref.	Debit	Credit	Balance

Depreciation Expense — Buses

Date	Explanation	Ref.	Debit	Credit	Balance

Interest Expense

Date	Explanation	Ref.	Debit	Credit	Balance

Name **Problem 3-1A Concluded**

Section

Date **Midwest Tours**

(c)

MIDWEST TOURS
Adjusted Trial Balance
June 30, 1999

	Debit	Credit

Name **Problem 3-2A**

Section

Date **Super Motel**

(a) General Journal J1

Date	Account Titles and Explanation	Ref.	Debit	Credit

(b)

Cash

Date	Explanation	Ref.	Debit	Credit	Balance

Prepaid Insurance

Date	Explanation	Ref.	Debit	Credit	Balance

Supplies

Date	Explanation	Ref.	Debit	Credit	Balance

Land

Date	Explanation	Ref.	Debit	Credit	Balance

Lodge

Date	Explanation	Ref.	Debit	Credit	Balance

Accumulated Depreciation — Lodge

Date	Explanation	Ref.	Debit	Credit	Balance

Furniture

Date	Explanation	Ref.	Debit	Credit	Balance

(b) (Continued)

Accumulated Depreciation — Furniture

Date	Explanation	Ref.	Debit	Credit	Balance

Accounts Payable

Date	Explanation	Ref.	Debit	Credit	Balance

Unearned Rent Revenue

Date	Explanation	Ref.	Debit	Credit	Balance

Salaries Payable

Date	Explanation	Ref.	Debit	Credit	Balance

Interest Payable

Date	Explanation	Ref.	Debit	Credit	Balance

Mortgage Payable

Date	Explanation	Ref.	Debit	Credit	Balance

Sara Sulton, Capital

Date	Explanation	Ref.	Debit	Credit	Balance

(b) (Continued)

Rent Revenue

Date	Explanation	Ref.	Debit	Credit	Balance

Salaries Expense

Date	Explanation	Ref.	Debit	Credit	Balance

Utilities Expense

Date	Explanation	Ref.	Debit	Credit	Balance

Advertising Expense

Date	Explanation	Ref.	Debit	Credit	Balance

Interest Expense

Date	Explanation	Ref.	Debit	Credit	Balance

Insurance Expense

Date	Explanation	Ref.	Debit	Credit	Balance

Supplies Expense

Date	Explanation	Ref.	Debit	Credit	Balance

Name **Problem 3-2A Continued**

Section

Date **Super Motel**

(b) (Continued)

Depreciation Expense — Lodge

Date	Explanation	Ref.	Debit	Credit	Balance

Depreciation Expense — Furniture

Date	Explanation	Ref.	Debit	Credit	Balance

(c)

SUPER MOTEL
Adjusted Trial Balance
May 31, 1999

	Debit	Credit

Name
Section
Date

Problem 3-2A Continued

Super Motel

(d)

SUPER MOTEL
Income Statement
For the Month Ended May 31, 1999

SUPER MOTEL
Owner's Equity Statement
For the Month Ended May 31, 1999

(d) (Continued)

SUPER MOTEL
Balance Sheet
May 31, 1999

Assets

Liabilities and Owner's Equity

Name **Problem 3-3A**

Section

Date **Irabu Co.**

(a) General Journal

Date	Account Titles and Explanation	Ref.	Debit	Credit

(b)

IRABU CO.

Income Statement

For the Quarter Ended September 30, 1999

Name

Section

Date

Problem 3-3A Concluded

Irabu Co.

(b) (Continued)

IRABU CO.
Owner's Equity Statement
For the Quarter Ended September 30, 1999

IRABU CO.
Balance Sheet
September 30, 1999

Assets

Liabilities and Owner's Equity

(c)

Name **Problem 3-4A**

Section

Date **Davis Company**

General Journal

	Date	Account Titles and Explanation	Ref.	Debit	Credit	
1						1
2						2
3						3
4						4
5						5
6						6
7						7
8						8
9						9
10						10
11						11
12						12
13						13
14						14
15						15
16						16
17						17
18						18
19						19
20						20
21						21
22						22
23						23
24						24
25						25
26						26
27						27
28						28
29						29
30						30
31						31
32						32
33						33
34						34
35						35
36						36
37						37
38						38
39						39
40						40

Name **Problem 3-5A**

Section

Date **Delino Equipment Repair**

(a), (c) and (e)

Cash No. 101

Date	Explanation	Ref.	Debit	Credit	Balance

Accounts Receivable No. 112

Date	Explanation	Ref.	Debit	Credit	Balance

Supplies No. 126

Date	Explanation	Ref.	Debit	Credit	Balance

Store Equipment No. 153

Date	Explanation	Ref.	Debit	Credit	Balance

Accumulated Depreciation — Store Equipment No. 154

Date	Explanation	Ref.	Debit	Credit	Balance

Name

Section

Date

Problem 3-5A Continued

Delino Equipment Repair

(a), (c) and (e) (Continued)

Accounts Payable — No. 201

Date	Explanation	Ref.	Debit	Credit	Balance

Unearned Service Revenue — No. 209

Date	Explanation	Ref.	Debit	Credit	Balance

Salaries Payable — No. 212

Date	Explanation	Ref.	Debit	Credit	Balance

P. Delino, Capital — No. 301

Date	Explanation	Ref.	Debit	Credit	Balance

Service Revenue — No. 407

Date	Explanation	Ref.	Debit	Credit	Balance

Depreciation Expense — No. 615

Date	Explanation	Ref.	Debit	Credit	Balance

(a), (c) and (e) (Continued)

Supplies Expense No. 631

Date	Explanation	Ref.	Debit	Credit	Balance

Salaries Expense No. 726

Date	Explanation	Ref.	Debit	Credit	Balance

Rent Expense No. 729

Date	Explanation	Ref.	Debit	Credit	Balance

(b) General Journal J1

	Date	Account Titles and Explanation	Ref.	Debit	Credit	
1						1
2						2
3						3
4						4
5						5
6						6
7						7
8						8
9						9
10						10
11						11
12						12
13						13
14						14
15						15
16						16
17						17
18						18
19						19
20						20

(b) (Continued) General Journal J1

Date	Account Titles and Explanation	Ref.	Debit	Credit

(e) General Journal J2

Date	Account Titles and Explanation	Ref.	Debit	Credit

Name

Section

Date

Problem 3-5A Continued

Delino Equipment Repair

(d) and (f)

DELINO EQUIPMENT REPAIR

Trial Balances

November 30, 1999

	Before Adjustment		After Adjustment	
	Dr.	Cr.	Dr.	Cr.
1				
2				
3				
4				
5				
6				
7				
8				
9				
10				
11				
12				
13				
14				
15				
16				
17				
18				
19				
20				

(g)

DELINO EQUIPMENT REPAIR

Income Statement

For the Month Ended November 30, 1999

1		
2		
3		
4		
5		
6		
7		
8		
9		
10		
11		
12		
13		
14		
15		

(g) (Continued)

DELINO EQUIPMENT REPAIR
Owner's Equity Statement
For the Month Ended November 30, 1999

DELINO EQUIPMENT REPAIR
Balance Sheet
November 30, 1999

Assets

Liabilities and Owner's Equity

Name *Problem 3-6A**

Section

Date **Cordero Graphics Company**

(a) General Journal

Date	Account Titles and Explanation	Ref.	Debit	Credit

(b)

CORDERO GRAPHICS COMPANY
Adjusted Trial Balance
June 30, 1999

	Debit	Credit

(c)

CORDERO GRAPHICS COMPANY
Income Statement
For the Six Months Ended June 30, 1999

(c) (Continued)

CORDERO GRAPHICS COMPANY
Owner's Equity Statement
For the Six Months Ended June 30, 1999

CORDERO GRAPHICS COMPANY
Balance Sheet
June 30, 1999

Assets

Liabilities and Owner's Equity

Name

Section

Date

Problem 3-1B

Orosco Security Service

(a) General Journal J15

	Date	Account Titles and Explanation	Ref.	Debit	Credit	
1						1
2						2
3						3
4						4
5						5
6						6
7						7
8						8
9						9
10						10
11						11
12						12
13						13
14						14
15						15
16						16
17						17
18						18
19						19
20						20
21						21
22						22
23						23
24						24
25						25
26						26
27						27
28						28
29						29
30						30
31						31
32						32
33						33
34						34
35						35
36						36
37						37
38						38
39						39
40						40

Name **Problem 3-1B Continued**

Section

Date **Orosco Security Service**

(b)

Cash

Date	Explanation	Ref.	Debit	Credit	Balance

Accounts Receivable

Date	Explanation	Ref.	Debit	Credit	Balance

Prepaid Insurance

Date	Explanation	Ref.	Debit	Credit	Balance

Automobiles

Date	Explanation	Ref.	Debit	Credit	Balance

Accumulated Depreciation — Automobiles

Date	Explanation	Ref.	Debit	Credit	Balance

Notes Payable

Date	Explanation	Ref.	Debit	Credit	Balance

Accounts Payable

Date	Explanation	Ref.	Debit	Credit	Balance

(b) (Continued)

Interest Payable

Date	Explanation	Ref.	Debit	Credit	Balance

Salaries Payable

Date	Explanation	Ref.	Debit	Credit	Balance

Unearned Revenue

Date	Explanation	Ref.	Debit	Credit	Balance

C. Orosco, Capital

Date	Explanation	Ref.	Debit	Credit	Balance

Service Revenue

Date	Explanation	Ref.	Debit	Credit	Balance

Salaries Expense

Date	Explanation	Ref.	Debit	Credit	Balance

Name | **Problem 3-1B Continued**

Section

Date | **Orosco Security Service**

(b) (Continued)

Repair Expense

Date	Explanation	Ref.	Debit	Credit	Balance

Gas and Oil Expense

Date	Explanation	Ref.	Debit	Credit	Balance

Insurance Expense

Date	Explanation	Ref.	Debit	Credit	Balance

Depreciation Expense — Automobiles

Date	Explanation	Ref.	Debit	Credit	Balance

Interest Expense

Date	Explanation	Ref.	Debit	Credit	Balance

Name **Problem 3-1B Concluded**

Section

Date **Orosco Security Service**

(c)

OROSCO SECURITY SERVICE
Adjusted Trial Balance
December 31, 1999

	Debit	Credit

Name **Problem 3-2B**

Section

Date **Spring River Resort**

(a) General Journal

	Date	Account Titles and Explanation	Ref.	Debit	Credit	
1						1
2						2
3						3
4						4
5						5
6						6
7						7
8						8
9						9
10						10
11						11
12						12
13						13
14						14
15						15
16						16
17						17
18						18
19						19
20						20
21						21
22						22
23						23
24						24
25						25
26						26
27						27
28						28
29						29
30						30
31						31
32						32
33						33
34						34
35						35
36						36
37						37
38						38
39						39
40						40

(b)

Cash

Date	Explanation	Ref.	Debit	Credit	Balance

Accounts Receivable

Date	Explanation	Ref.	Debit	Credit	Balance

Prepaid Insurance

Date	Explanation	Ref.	Debit	Credit	Balance

Supplies

Date	Explanation	Ref.	Debit	Credit	Balance

Land

Date	Explanation	Ref.	Debit	Credit	Balance

Cottages

Date	Explanation	Ref.	Debit	Credit	Balance

Accumulated Depreciation — Cottages

Date	Explanation	Ref.	Debit	Credit	Balance

(b) (Continued)

Furniture

Date	Explanation	Ref.	Debit	Credit	Balance

Accumulated Depreciation — Furniture

Date	Explanation	Ref.	Debit	Credit	Balance

Accounts Payable

Date	Explanation	Ref.	Debit	Credit	Balance

Unearned Rent Revenue

Date	Explanation	Ref.	Debit	Credit	Balance

Salaries Payable

Date	Explanation	Ref.	Debit	Credit	Balance

Interest Payable

Date	Explanation	Ref.	Debit	Credit	Balance

Mortgage Payable

Date	Explanation	Ref.	Debit	Credit	Balance

(b) (Continued)

P. Villone, Capital

Date	Explanation	Ref.	Debit	Credit	Balance

P. Villone, Drawing

Date	Explanation	Ref.	Debit	Credit	Balance

Rent Revenue

Date	Explanation	Ref.	Debit	Credit	Balance

Salaries Expense

Date	Explanation	Ref.	Debit	Credit	Balance

Utilities Expense

Date	Explanation	Ref.	Debit	Credit	Balance

Repair Expense

Date	Explanation	Ref.	Debit	Credit	Balance

Insurance Expense

Date	Explanation	Ref.	Debit	Credit	Balance

(b) (Continued)

Supplies Expense

Date	Explanation	Ref.	Debit	Credit	Balance

Depreciation Expense — Cottages

Date	Explanation	Ref.	Debit	Credit	Balance

Depreciation Expense — Furniture

Date	Explanation	Ref.	Debit	Credit	Balance

Interest Expense

Date	Explanation	Ref.	Debit	Credit	Balance

Name Problem 3-2B Continued

Section

Date Spring River Resort

(c)

SPRING RIVER RESORT
Adjusted Trial Balance
August 31, 1999

	Debit	Credit

Name | **Problem 3-2B Continued**
Section
Date | **Spring River Resort**

(d)

SPRING RIVER RESORT
Income Statement
For the Three Months Ended August 31, 1999

SPRING RIVER RESORT
Owner's Equity Statement
For the Three Months Ended August 31, 1999

Name | **Problem 3-2B Concluded**

Section

Date | **Spring River Resort**

(d) (Continued)

SPRING RIVER RESORT

Balance Sheet

August 31, 1999

Assets

Liabilities and Owner's Equity

Name | **Problem 3-3B**

Section

Date | **Yount Advertising Agency**

(a) General Journal

Date	Account Titles and Explanation	Ref.	Debit	Credit

(b)

YOUNT ADVERTISING AGENCY

Income Statement

For the Year Ended December 31, 1999

(b) (Continued)

YOUNT ADVERTISING AGENCY
Owner's Equity Statement
For the Year Ended December 31, 1999

YOUNT ADVERTISING AGENCY
Balance Sheet
December 31, 1999

Assets

Liabilities and Owner's Equity

(c)

(1)

(2)

Name **Problem 3-4B**

Section

Date **Oklahoma Company**

General Journal

Date	Account Titles and Explanation	Ref.	Debit	Credit

Name **Problem 3-5B**

Section

Date **Silva Equipment Repair**

(a), (c) and (e)

Cash No. 101

Date	Explanation	Ref.	Debit	Credit	Balance

Accounts Receivable No. 112

Date	Explanation	Ref.	Debit	Credit	Balance

Supplies No. 126

Date	Explanation	Ref.	Debit	Credit	Balance

Store Equipment No. 153

Date	Explanation	Ref.	Debit	Credit	Balance

Accumulated Depreciation – Store Equipment No. 154

Date	Explanation	Ref.	Debit	Credit	Balance

Name | Problem 3-5B Continued

Section

Date | Silva Equipment Repair

(a), (c) and (e) (Continued)

Accounts Payable | No. 201

Date	Explanation	Ref.	Debit	Credit	Balance

Unearned Service Revenue | No. 209

Date	Explanation	Ref.	Debit	Credit	Balance

Salaries Payable | No. 212

Date	Explanation	Ref.	Debit	Credit	Balance

J. Silva, Capital | No. 301

Date	Explanation	Ref.	Debit	Credit	Balance

Service Revenue | No. 407

Date	Explanation	Ref.	Debit	Credit	Balance

Depreciation Expense | No. 615

Date	Explanation	Ref.	Debit	Credit	Balance

Name

Section

Date

Problem 3-5B Continued

Silva Equipment Repair

(a), (c) and (e) (Continued)

Supplies Expense — No. 615

Date	Explanation	Ref.	Debit	Credit	Balance

Salaries Expense — No. 726

Date	Explanation	Ref.	Debit	Credit	Balance

Rent Expense — No. 729

Date	Explanation	Ref.	Debit	Credit	Balance

(b)

General Journal — J1

	Date	Account Titles and Explanation	Ref.	Debit	Credit	
1						1
2						2
3						3
4						4
5						5
6						6
7						7
8						8
9						9
10						10
11						11
12						12
13						13
14						14
15						15
16						16
17						17
18						18
19						19
20						20

Name
Section
Date

Problem 3-5B Continued

Silva Equipment Repair

(b)(Continued) General Journal J1

	Date	Account Titles and Explanation	Ref.	Debit	Credit	
1						1
2						2
3						3
4						4
5						5
6						6
7						7
8						8
9						9
10						10
11						11
12						12
13						13
14						14
15						15
16						16
17						17

(e) General Journal J2

	Date	Account Titles and Explanation	Ref.	Debit	Credit	
1						1
2						2
3						3
4						4
5						5
6						6
7						7
8						8
9						9
10						10
11						11
12						12
13						13
14						14
15						15
16						16

(d) and (f)

SILVA EQUIPMENT REPAIR
Trial Balances
September 30, 1999

	Before Adjustment		After Adjustment	
	Dr.	Cr.	Dr.	Cr.
1				
2				
3				
4				
5				
6				
7				
8				
9				
10				
11				
12				
13				
14				
15				
16				
17				
18				
19				
20				

(g)

SILVA EQUIPMENT REPAIR
Income Statement
For the Month Ended September 30, 1999

1		
2		
3		
4		
5		
6		
7		
8		
9		
10		
11		
12		
13		
14		
15		

(g) (Continued)

SILVA EQUIPMENT REPAIR
Owner's Equity Statement
For the Month Ended September 30, 1999

SILVA EQUIPMENT REPAIR
Balance Sheet
September 30, 1999

Assets

Liabilities and Owner's Equity

Name

Section

Date

(a)

(b)

(c)

Name

Section

Date

Chapter 3 Comparative Analysis Problem

Kellogg vs. General Mills

	Kellogg	General Mills
Increase (decrease) from 1996 to 1997		
(in thousands) in		
(a) Property, plant, and equipment, net		
(b) Selling, general, and administrative expense		
(c) Accounts payable		
(d) Net income		
(e) Cash and cash equivalents		

Name

Section

Date

Smith's Food and Drug Centers, Inc.

(a)

(b)

(a)

HAPPY TRAVEL COURT
Income Statement
For the Quarter Ended March 31, 1999

(b)

REAL-WORLD FOCUS Laser Recording Systems Incorporated

(a)

(b)

(c)

ETHICS CASE Die Hard Company

(a)

(b)

(c)

Name

Section

Date

Name
Section
Date

Warren Company

WARREN COMPANY
Work Sheet

	Account Titles	Trial Balance		Adjusting Entries		Adjusted Trial Balance		Income Statement		Balance Sheet		
		Debit	Credit	Debit	Credit	Debit	Credit	Debit	Credit	Debit	Credit	
1												1
2												2
3												3
4												4
5												5
6												6
7												7
8												8
9												9
10												10
11												11
12												12
13												13
14												14
15												15
16												16
17												17
18												18
19												19
20												20
21												21
22												22
23												23
24												24

Name

Section

Date

Date	Explanation	Ref.	Debit	Credit	Balance

Date	Explanation	Ref.	Debit	Credit	Balance

Name

Section

Date

Name

Section

Date

Name | **Exercise 4-1**

Section

Date | **Jose Navarro Company**

JOSE NAVARRO COMPANY

Work Sheet (Partial)

For the Month Ended April 30, 1999

	Account Titles	Adjusted Trial Balance Dr.	Adjusted Trial Balance Cr.	Income Statement Dr.	Income Statement Cr.	Balance Sheet Dr.	Balance Sheet Cr.	
1								1
2								2
3								3
4								4
5								5
6								6
7								7
8								8
9								9
10								10
11								11
12								12
13								13
14								14
15								15
16								16
17								17
18								18
19								19
20								20
21								21
22								22
23								23
24								24
25								25

Name

Section

Date

Exercise 4-2

Jose Navarro Company

JOSE NAVARRO COMPANY

Income Statement

For the Month Ended April 30, 1999

JOSE NAVARRO COMPANY

Owner's Equity Statement

For the Month Ended April 30, 1999

JOSE NAVARRO COMPANY

Balance Sheet

April 30, 1999

Assets

Liabilities and Owner's Equity

Name　　　　　　　　　　　　　　　　　　　　　　　　　　　　　　**Exercise 4-3**

Section

Date　　　　　　　　　　　　　　　　　　　　　　　　　　　　　　**Jose Navarro Company**

(a)

(b)

INCOME SUMMARY			J. NAVARRO, CAPITAL	

(c)

JOSE NAVARRO COMPANY
Post-Closing Trial Balance
April 30, 1999

	Debit	Credit

Name

Exercises 4-4 to 4-5

Section

Date

#4

#5

Name **Exercise 4-6**

Section

Date **Raphael Company**

(a)

General Journal

Date	Account Titles and Explanation	Ref.	Debit	Credit

(b)

S. Raphael, Capital No. 301

Date	Explanation	Ref.	Debit	Credit	Balance

Income Summary No. 350

Date	Explanation	Ref.	Debit	Credit	Balance

(c)

RAPHAEL COMPANY

Post-Closing Trial Balance

July 31, 1999

	Debit	Credit

Name | **Exercise 4-7**

Section

Date | **Raphael Company**

(a)

RAPHAEL COMPANY
Income Statement
For the Year Ended July 31, 1999

RAPHAEL COMPANY
Owner's Equity Statement
For the Year Ended July 31, 1999

(b)

RAPHAEL COMPANY
Balance Sheet
July 31, 1999

Assets

Liabilities and Owner's Equity

Name

Section

Date

#8

(a)

(b)

INCOME SUMMARY

#9

	Debit	Credit
Cash	270	
Accounts payable		270
Supplies	600	
Accounts payable		540
Equipment		60
Debit draw	400	
Salaries Expense		400

Name | **Exercise 4-10**

Section

Date | **Bel-Air Bowling Alley**

(a)

BEL-AIR BOWLING ALLEY

Balance Sheet

December 31, 1999

Assets

Liabilities and Owner's Equity

(b)

Name

Section

Date

***Exercise 4-11**

Garrett Employment Agency

(a)

(b)

(c/e)

ACCOUNTS RECEIVABLE	
4000	

COMMISSION REVENUE	
	4000

INTEREST PAYABLE	
	2000

INTEREST EXPENSE	
2000	

(d)

Additional working papers for this problem are at the back of this book.

(b)

SPELLMAN ROOFING
Income Statement
For the Month Ended March 31, 1999

SPELLMAN ROOFING
Owner's Equity Statement
For the Month Ended March 31, 1999

(b) (Continued)

SPELLMAN ROOFING
Balance Sheet
March 31, 1999

Assets	
Liabilities and Owner's Equity	

Name	Problem 4-1A Concluded
Section	
Date	Spellman Roofing

(c) General Journal

Date	Account Titles and Explanation	Ref.	Debit	Credit
	Adjusting Entries			

(d) General Journal

Date	Account Titles and Explanation	Ref.	Debit	Credit
	Closing Entries			

Name

Section

Date

Problem 4-2A

Perez Company

(a)

PEREZ COMPANY
Work Sheet (Partial)
For the Year Ended December 31, 1999

	Account		Adjusted Trial Balance		Income Statement		Balance Sheet	
	No.	Title	Dr.	Cr.	Dr.	Cr.	Dr.	Cr.
1								
2								
3								
4								
5								
6								
7								
8								
9								
10								
11								
12								
13								
14								
15								
16								
17								
18								
19								
20								
21								
22								
23								
24								
25								
26								
27								
28								

(b)

PEREZ COMPANY
Income Statement
For the Year Ended December 31, 1999

PEREZ COMPANY
Owner's Equity Statement
For the Year Ended December 31, 1999

Name

Section

Date

Problem 4-2A Continued

Perez Company

(b) (Continued)

PEREZ COMPANY

Balance Sheet

December 31, 1999

Assets

Liabilities and Owner's Equity

Name | **Problem 4-2A Continued**

Section

Date | **Perez Company**

(c) General Journal J14

	Date	Account Titles and Explanation	Ref.	Debit	Credit	
1		Closing Entries				1
2						2
3						3
4						4
5						5
6						6
7						7
8						8
9						9
10						10
11						11
12						12
13						13
14						14
15						15
16						16
17						17
18						18

(d) J. Perez, Capital No. 301

Date	Explanation	Ref.	Debit	Credit	Balance

J. Perez, Drawing No. 306

Date	Explanation	Ref.	Debit	Credit	Balance

Income Summary No. 350

Date	Explanation	Ref.	Debit	Credit	Balance

Name

Section

Date

Problem 4-2A Continued

Perez Company

(d) (Continued)

Service Revenue — No. 400

Date	Explanation	Ref.	Debit	Credit	Balance

Advertising Expense — No. 610

Date	Explanation	Ref.	Debit	Credit	Balance

Supplies Expense — No. 631

Date	Explanation	Ref.	Debit	Credit	Balance

Depreciation Expense — No. 711

Date	Explanation	Ref.	Debit	Credit	Balance

Interest Expense — No. 718

Date	Explanation	Ref.	Debit	Credit	Balance

Insurance Expense — No. 722

Date	Explanation	Ref.	Debit	Credit	Balance

Name | **Problem 4-2A Concluded**

Section

Date | **Perez Company**

(d) (Continued)

Salaries Expense — No. 726

Date	Explanation	Ref.	Debit	Credit	Balance

(e)

PERZ COMPANY

Post-Closing Trial Balance

December 31, 1999

		Debit	Credit	
1				1
2				2
3				3
4				4
5				5
6				6
7				7
8				8
9				9
10				10
11				11
12				12
13				13
14				14
15				15
16				16
17				17
18				18
19				19
20				20

Name

Section

Date

Problem 4-3A

Strug Company

(a)

STRUG COMPANY
Income Statement
For the Year Ended December 31, 1999

STRUG COMPANY
Balance Sheet
December 31, 1999

Assets

Liabilities and Owner's Equity

Name

Section

Date

(a) (Continued)

STRUG COMPANY

Owner's Equity Statement

For the Year Ended December 31, 1999

(b) General Journal

Date	Account Titles	Ref.	Debit	Credit
	Closing Entries			

(c) General Ledger Accounts

K. Strug, Capital	No. 301

Repair Expense	No. 622

Depreciation Expense	No. 711

K. Strug, Drawing	No. 306

Insurance Expense	No. 722

Income Summary	No. 350

Salaries Expense	No. 726

Service Revenue	No. 400

Utilities Expense	No. 732

(d)

STRUG COMPANY
Post-Closing Trial Balance
December 31, 1999

	Debit	Credit

Name

Section

Date

Problem 4-4A Continued

Logan Management Services

Additional working papers for this problem are at the back of this book.

(b)

LOGAN MANAGEMENT SERVICES

Balance Sheet

December 31, 1999

Assets

Liabilities and Owner's Equity

Name

Section

Date

Problem 4-4A Continued

Logan Management Services

(c) and (d) General Journal

Date	Account Titles and Explanation	Ref.	Debit	Credit
(c)	Adjusting Entries			
(d)	Closing Entries			

LOGAN MANAGEMENT SERVICES
Post-Closing Trial Balance
December 31, 1999

(e)

	Debit	Credit

Name

Section

Date

Problem 4-5A

Jill's Window Washing

(a) General Journal J1

Date	Account Titles and Explanation	Ref.	Debit	Credit

Name | **Problem 4-5A Continued**

Section

Date | **Jill's Window Washing**

(a), (e) and (f)

Cash — No. 101

Date	Explanation	Ref.	Debit	Credit	Balance

Accounts Receivable — No. 112

Date	Explanation	Ref.	Debit	Credit	Balance

Cleaning Supplies — No. 128

Date	Explanation	Ref.	Debit	Credit	Balance

Prepaid Insurance — No. 130

Date	Explanation	Ref.	Debit	Credit	Balance

Equipment — No. 157

Date	Explanation	Ref.	Debit	Credit	Balance

(a), (e) and (f) (Continued)

Accumulated Depreciation — Equipment — No. 158

Date	Explanation	Ref.	Debit	Credit	Balance

Accounts Payable — No. 201

Date	Explanation	Ref.	Debit	Credit	Balance

Salaries Payable — No. 212

Date	Explanation	Ref.	Debit	Credit	Balance

Jill Marsh, Capital — No. 301

Date	Explanation	Ref.	Debit	Credit	Balance

Jill Marsh, Drawing — No. 306

Date	Explanation	Ref.	Debit	Credit	Balance

Income Summary — No. 350

Date	Explanation	Ref.	Debit	Credit	Balance

Name **Problem 4-5A Continued**

Section

Date **Jill's Window Washing**

(a), (e) and (f) (Continued)

Service Revenue No. 400

Date	Explanation	Ref.	Debit	Credit	Balance

Gas & Oil Expense No. 633

Date	Explanation	Ref.	Debit	Credit	Balance

Cleaning Supplies Expense No. 634

Date	Explanation	Ref.	Debit	Credit	Balance

Depreciation Expense No. 711

Date	Explanation	Ref.	Debit	Credit	Balance

Insurance Expense No. 722

Date	Explanation	Ref.	Debit	Credit	Balance

Salaries Expense No. 726

Date	Explanation	Ref.	Debit	Credit	Balance

Additional working papers for this problem are at the back of this book.

(d)

JILL'S WINDOW WASHING
Income Statement
For the Month Ended July 31, 1999

JILL'S WINDOW WASHING
Owner's Equity Statement
For the Month Ended July 31, 1999

(d) (Continued)

JILL'S WINDOW WASHING
Balance Sheet
July 31, 1999

1	Assets		
2			
3			
4			
5			
6			
7			
8			
9			
10			
11			
12			
13			
14	Liabilities and Owner's Equity		
15			
16			
17			
18			
19			
20			
21			
22			

(g)

JILL'S WINDOW WASHING
Post-Closing Trial Balance
July 31, 1999

		Debit	Credit
1			
2			
3			
4			
5			
6			
7			
8			
9			
10			
11			
12			

Name | **Problem 4-5A Concluded**

Section

Date | **Jill's Window Washing**

(e) and (f) General Journal J2–J3

	Date	Account Titles and Explanation	Ref.	Debit	Credit	
1	(e)	Adjusting Entries				1
2						2
3						3
4						4
5						5
6						6
7						7
8						8
9						9
10						10
11						11
12						12
13						13
14						14
15						15
16						16
17						17
18						18
19						19
20						20
21	(f)	Closing Entries				21
22						22
23						23
24						24
25						25
26						26
27						27
28						28
29						29
30						30
31						31
32						32
33						33
34						34
35						35
36						36
37						37
38						38
39						39
40						40

Name

Section

Date

Additional working papers for this problem are at the back of this book.

(b)

EVERLAST TV REPAIR

Trial Balance

April 30, 1999

	Debit	Credit

Name | **Problem 4-1B Continued**

Section

Date | **Columbo P.I.**

Additional working papers for this problem are at the back of this book.

(b)

COLUMBO P.I.
Income Statement
For the Quarter Ended March 31, 1999

1			1
2			2
3			3
4			4
5			5
6			6
7			7
8			8
9			9
10			10
11			11
12			12
13			13
14			14
15			15

COLUMBO P.I.
Owner's Equity Statement
For the Quarter Ended March 31, 1999

1			1
2			2
3			3
4			4
5			5
6			6
7			7
8			8
9			9
10			10

(b) (Continued)

COLUMBO P.I.
Balance Sheet
March 31, 1999

1	Assets		1
2			2
3			3
4			4
5			5
6			6
7			7
8			8
9			9
10			10
11			11
12			12
13			13
14			14
15			15
16	Liabilities and Owner's Equity		16
17			17
18			18
19			19
20			20
21			21
22			22
23			23
24			24
25			25
26			26
27			27
28			28
29			29
30			30

(c) General Journal

	Date	Account Titles and Explanation	Ref.	Debit	Credit
1		Adjusting Entries			
2					
3					
4					
5					
6					
7					
8					
9					
10					
11					
12					
13					
14					
15					
16					

(d) General Journal

	Date	Account Titles and Explanation	Ref.	Debit	Credit
1		Closing Entries			
2					
3					
4					
5					
6					
7					
8					
9					
10					
11					
12					
13					
14					
15					
16					
17					
18					
19					

Name **Problem 4-2B**

Section

Date **Oslo Company**

(a)

OSLO COMPANY

Work Sheet (Partial)

For the Year Ended December 31, 1999

Account		Adjusted Trial Balance		Income Statement		Balance Sheet	
No.	Titles	Dr.	Cr.	Dr.	Cr.	Dr.	Cr.

Name | **Problem 4-2B Continued**

Section

Date | **Oslo Company**

(b)

OSLO COMPANY

Income Statement

For the Year Ended December 31, 1999

OSLO COMPANY

Owner's Equity Statement

For the Year Ended December 31, 1999

(b) (Continued)

OSLO COMPANY
Balance Sheet
December 31, 1999

Assets

Liabilities and Owner's Equity

Name

Section

Date

Problem 4-2B Continued

Oslo Company

(c) General Journal J14

Date	Account Titles and Explanation	Ref.	Debit	Credit
	Closing Entries			

(d)

S. Oslo, Capital No. 301

Date	Explanation	Ref.	Debit	Credit	Balance

S. Oslo, Drawing No. 306

Date	Explanation	Ref.	Debit	Credit	Balance

Income Summary No. 350

Date	Explanation	Ref.	Debit	Credit	Balance

Service Revenue No. 400

Date	Explanation	Ref.	Debit	Credit	Balance

Advertising Expense No. 610

Date	Explanation	Ref.	Debit	Credit	Balance

Supplies Expense No. 631

Date	Explanation	Ref.	Debit	Credit	Balance

(d) (Continued)

Depreciation Expense — No. 711

Date	Explanation	Ref.	Debit	Credit	Balance

Insurance Expense — No. 722

Date	Explanation	Ref.	Debit	Credit	Balance

Salaries Expense — No. 726

Date	Explanation	Ref.	Debit	Credit	Balance

Interest Expense — No. 905

Date	Explanation	Ref.	Debit	Credit	Balance

(e)

OSLO COMPANY
Post-Closing Trial Balance
December 31, 1999

		Debit	Credit	
1				1
2				2
3				3
4				4
5				5
6				6
7				7
8				8
9				9
10				10
11				11
12				12
13				13
14				14

Name **Problem 4-3B**

Section

Date **Sierra Company**

(a)

SIERRA COMPANY
Income Statement
For the Year Ended December 31, 1999

1		
2		
3		
4		
5		
6		
7		
8		
9		
10		
11		
12		
13		
14		
15		

SIERRA COMPANY
Owner's Equity Statement
For the Year Ended December 31, 1999

1		
2		
3		
4		
5		
6		
7		
8		
9		
10		

(a) (Continued)

SIERRA COMPANY
Balance Sheet
December 31, 1999

Assets

Liabilities and Owner's Equity

(b) General Journal

Date	Account Titles and Explanation	Ref.	Debit	Credit

(c) General Ledger Accounts

M. Sierra, Capital No. 301

Repair Expense No. 622

Depreciation Expense No. 711

M. Sierra, Drawing No. 306

Insurance Expense No. 722

Income Summary No. 350

Salaries Expense No. 726

Service Revenue No. 400

Utilities Expense No. 732

(d)

SIERRA COMPANY
Post-Closing Trial Balance
December 31, 1999

	Debit	Credit

Name **Problem 4-4B Continued**

Section

Date **Waterworld Amusement Park**

Additional working papers for this problem are at the back of this book.

(b)

WATERWORLD AMUSEMENT PARK

Balance Sheet

September 30, 1999

Assets		
Liabilities and Owner's Equity		

(c) and (d) General Journal

Date	Account Titles and Explanation	Ref.	Debit	Credit
(c)	Adjusting Entries			
(d)	Closing Entries			

(e)

WATERWORLD AMUSEMENT PARK
Post-Closing Trial Balance
September 30, 1999

	Debit	Credit

Name | **Problem 4-5B**

Section

Date | **Anna's Carpet Cleaners**

Additional working papers for this problem are at the back of this book.

(a) General Journal J1

Date	Account Titles and Explanation	Ref.	Debit	Credit

Name
Section
Date

Problem 4-5B Continued

Anna's Carpet Cleaners

(a), (e) and (f)

Cash — No. 101

Date	Explanation	Ref.	Debit	Credit	Balance

Accounts Receivable — No. 112

Date	Explanation	Ref.	Debit	Credit	Balance

Cleaning Supplies — No. 128

Date	Explanation	Ref.	Debit	Credit	Balance

Prepaid Insurance — No. 130

Date	Explanation	Ref.	Debit	Credit	Balance

Equipment — No. 157

Date	Explanation	Ref.	Debit	Credit	Balance

Accumulated Depreciation—Equipment — No. 158

Date	Explanation	Ref.	Debit	Credit	Balance

(a), (e) and (f) (Continued)

Accounts Payable No. 201

Date	Explanation	Ref.	Debit	Credit	Balance

Salaries Payable No. 212

Date	Explanation	Ref.	Debit	Credit	Balance

A. Khan, Capital No. 301

Date	Explanation	Ref.	Debit	Credit	Balance

A. Khan, Drawing No. 306

Date	Explanation	Ref.	Debit	Credit	Balance

Income Summary No. 350

Date	Explanation	Ref.	Debit	Credit	Balance

Service Revenue No. 400

Date	Explanation	Ref.	Debit	Credit	Balance

Name

Section

Date

Problem 4-5B Continued

Anna's Carpet Cleaners

(a), (e) and (f) (Continued)

Gas & Oil Expense — No. 633

Date	Explanation	Ref.	Debit	Credit	Balance

Cleaning Supplies Expense — No. 634

Date	Explanation	Ref.	Debit	Credit	Balance

Depreciation Expense — No. 711

Date	Explanation	Ref.	Debit	Credit	Balance

Insurance Expense — No. 722

Date	Explanation	Ref.	Debit	Credit	Balance

Salaries Expense — No. 726

Date	Explanation	Ref.	Debit	Credit	Balance

Name

Section

Date

(d)

ANNA'S CARPET CLEANERS
Income Statement
For the Month Ended March 31, 1999

ANNA'S CARPET CLEANERS
Owner's Equity Statement
For the Month Ended March 31, 1999

(d) (Continued)

ANNA'S CARPET CLEANERS
Balance Sheet
March 31, 1999

Assets

Liabilities and Owner's Equity

(g)

ANNA'S CARPET CLEANERS
Post-Closing Trial Balance
March 31, 1999

	Debit	Credit

Name

Section

Date

Problem 4-5B Continued

Anna's Carpet Cleaners

(e) and (f) General Journal J2–J3

	Date	Account Titles and Explanation	Ref.	Debit	Credit	
1	(e)	Adjusting Entries				1
2						2
3						3
4						4
5						5
6						6
7						7
8						8
9						9
10						10
11						11
12						12
13						13
14						14
15						15
16						16
17						17
18						18
19						19
20						20
21	(f)	Closing Entries				21
22						22
23						23
24						24
25						25
26						26
27						27
28						28
29						29
30						30
31						31
32						32
33						33
34						34
35						35
36						36
37						37
38						38
39						39
40						40

Name

Section

Date

Kellogg Company

1.

2.

3.

4.

5.

Name

Section

Date

Kellogg vs. General Mills

	Kellogg	General Mills
(a) In millions		
1. Total current assets		
2. Net property, plant, and equipment		
3. Total current liabilities		
4. Total stockholders' (shareholders') equity		

(b)

Name

Section

Date

Case Corporation

(a), (b), and (c)

(a)

(b)

(c) General Ledger Account	Income Statement Item

Name

Section

Date

Case Corporation

(d)

Revenues	
Costs and expenses	
Income from operations before taxes	

Name

Section

Date

(a)

CLEANFAST JANITORIAL SERVICE

Balance Sheet

December 31, 1999

Assets

Liabilities and Owner's Equity

Calculation of adjusted capital balance:

Capital balance as reported	54000

(b)

Name

Section

Date

REAL-WORLD FOCUS Bethlehem Corporation

(a)

(b)

(c)

ETHICS CASE Magnus Perfume Company

(a)

(b)

(c)

Name

Section

Date

Name

Section

Date

Name

Section

Date

Name

Section

Date

General Journal

Date	Account Titles and Explanation	Debit	Credit
#1			
#4			

Name **Exercise 5-2**

Section

Date **College Office Supply**

General Journal

Date	Account Titles and Explanation	Ref.	Debit	Credit

Name **Exercise 5-3**

Section

Date **Arcadian Company**

General Journal

Date	Account Titles and Explanation	Ref.	Debit	Credit

Name

Section

Date

#5 (a)

LOPEZ COMPANY

Income Statement (Partial)

For the Year Ended October 31, 1999

1			
2			
3			
4			
5			
6			
7			

(b)

		Debit	Credit
1			
2			
3			
4			
5			
6			
7			

#6

		Debit	Credit
1			
2			
3			
4			
5			
6			
7			
8			
9			
10			
11			
12			
13			
14			
15			

Name

Section

Date

Exercise 5-7

Alvarez Company

ALVAREZ COMPANY
Work Sheet (Partial)
For the Period Ended May 31, 1999

	Account Titles	Adjusted Trial Balance		Income Statement		Balance Sheet		
		Dr.	Cr.	Dr.	Cr.	Dr.	Cr.	
1								1
2								2
3								3
4								4
5								5
6								6
7								7
8								8
9								9
10								10
11								11
12								12
13								13
14								14
15								15
16								16
17								17
18								18
19								19
20								20

Name **Exercise 5-8**

Section

Date **Acevedo Company**

(a)

ACEVEDO COMPANY

Income Statement

For the Year Ended December 31, 1999

(b)

ACEVEDO COMPANY

Income Statement

For the Year Ended December 31, 1999

Name

Section

Date

Exercises 5-9 to 5-10

#9

#10

Name **Problem 5-1A**

Section

Date **Carlos Hardware Store**

(a) General Journal

	Date	Account Titles and Explanation	Ref.	Debit	Credit	
1						1
2						2
3						3
4						4
5						5
6						6
7						7
8						8
9						9
10						10
11						11
12						12
13						13
14						14
15						15
16						16
17						17
18						18
19						19
20						20
21						21
22						22
23						23
24						24
25						25
26						26
27						27
28						28
29						29
30						30
31						31
32						32
33						33
34						34
35						35
36						36
37						37
38						38
39						39
40						40

Name

Section

Date

Problem 5-1A Continued

Carlos Hardware Store

(a) (Continued)

General Journal

	Date	Account Titles and Explanation	Ref.	Debit	Credit	
1						1
2						2
3						3
4						4
5						5
6						6
7						7
8						8
9						9
10						10
11						11
12						12
13						13
14						14
15						15
16						16

(b)

Cash No. 101

Date	Explanation	Ref.	Debit	Credit	Balance

Accounts Receivable No. 112

Date	Explanation	Ref.	Debit	Credit	Balance

Name

Section

Date

Problem 5-1A Continued

Carlos Hardware Store

(b) (Continued)

Merchandise Inventory — No. 120

Date	Explanation	Ref.	Debit	Credit	Balance

Supplies — No. 126

Date	Explanation	Ref.	Debit	Credit	Balance

Accounts Payable — No. 201

Date	Explanation	Ref.	Debit	Credit	Balance

J. Carlos, Capital — No. 301

Date	Explanation	Ref.	Debit	Credit	Balance

(b) (Continued)

Sales — No. 401

Date	Explanation	Ref.	Debit	Credit	Balance

Sales Returns and Allowances — No. 412

Date	Explanation	Ref.	Debit	Credit	Balance

Sales Discounts — No. 414

Date	Explanation	Ref.	Debit	Credit	Balance

Cost of Goods Sold — No. 505

Date	Explanation	Ref.	Debit	Credit	Balance

(c)

CARLOS HARDWARE STORE
Income Statement (Partial)
For the Month Ended May 31, 1999

Name

Section

Date

Problem 5-4A Continued

Rowbuck Department Store

(a) (Continued)

ROWBUCK DEPARTMENT STORE

Owner's Equity Statement

For the Year Ended November 30, 1999

ROWBUCK DEPARTMENT STORE

Balance Sheet

December 31, 1999

Assest

Liabilities and Owner's Equity

Name

Section

Date

Problem 5-4A Concluded

Rowbuck Department Store

(b) and (c)

General Journal

Date	Account Titles and Explanation	Ref.	Debit	Credit
(b)	Adjusting Entries			
(d)	Closing Entries			

Name Problem 5-5A

Section

Date Chi Chi's Pro Shop

(a)

General Journal

Date	Account Titles and Explanation	Ref.	Debit	Credit

Name

Section

Date

Problem 5-5A Continued

Chi Chi's Pro Shop

(b)

Cash — No. 101

Date	Explanation	Ref.	Debit	Credit	Balance

Accounts Receivable — No. 112

Date	Explanation	Ref.	Debit	Credit	Balance

Merchandise Inventory — No. 120

Date	Explanation	Ref.	Debit	Credit	Balance

Accounts Payable — No. 201

Date	Explanation	Ref.	Debit	Credit	Balance

Name

Section

Date

Problem 5-5A Concluded

Chi Chi's Pro Shop

(b) (Continued)

G. Garcia, Capital — No. 301

Date	Explanation	Ref.	Debit	Credit	Balance

Sales — No. 401

Date	Explanation	Ref.	Debit	Credit	Balance

Sales Returns and Allowances — No. 412

Date	Explanation	Ref.	Debit	Credit	Balance

Cost of Goods Sold — No. 505

Date	Explanation	Ref.	Debit	Credit	Balance

(c)

CHI CHI'S PRO SHOP
Trial Balance
April 30, 1999

		Debit	Credit	
1				1
2				2
3				3
4				4
5				5
6				6
7				7
8				8
9				9
10				10
11				11
12				12

Name

Section

Date

Problem 5-1B

Maggie Zine Distributing Company

(a)

General Journal

Date	Account Titles and Explanation	Ref.	Debit	Credit

Name

Section

Date

Maggie Zine Distributing Company

(a) (Continued)

General Journal

Date	Account Titles and Explanation	Ref.	Debit	Credit

(b)

Cash No. 101

Date	Explanation	Ref.	Debit	Credit	Balance

Accounts Receivable No. 112

Date	Explanation	Ref.	Debit	Credit	Balance

Name
Section
Date

Problem 5-1B Continued

Maggie Zine Distributing Company

(b) (Continued)

Merchandise Inventory — No. 120

Date	Explanation	Ref.	Debit	Credit	Balance

Accounts Payable — No. 201

Date	Explanation	Ref.	Debit	Credit	Balance

M. Zine, Capital — No. 301

Date	Explanation	Ref.	Debit	Credit	Balance

Sales — No. 401

Date	Explanation	Ref.	Debit	Credit	Balance

(b) (Continued)

Sales Returns and Allowances — No. 412

Date	Explanation	Ref.	Debit	Credit	Balance

Sales Discounts — No. 414

Date	Explanation	Ref.	Debit	Credit	Balance

Cost of Goods Sold — No. 505

Date	Explanation	Ref.	Debit	Credit	Balance

Freight-out — No. 644

Date	Explanation	Ref.	Debit	Credit	Balance

(c)

MAGGIE ZINE DISTRIBUTING COMPANY
Income Statement (Partial)
For the Month Ended April 30, 1999

1				1
2				2
3				3
4				4
5				5
6				6
7				7
8				8
9				9
10				10

Name

Section

Date

Problem 5-2B

Tom E. Hawks Auto Sales

General Journal

Date	Account Titles and Explanation	Ref.	Debit	Credit

Name | **Problem 5-3B Continued**

Section

Date | **Cal. A. Fornia Fashion Center**

Additional working papers for this problem are at the back of this book.

(b)

CAL. A. FORNIA FASHION CENTER

Income Statement

For the Year Ended December 31, 1999

Name

Section

Date

Problem 5-3B Continued

Cal. A. Fornia Fashion Center

(b) (Continued)

CAL. A. FORNIA FASHION CENTER

Owner's Equity Statement

For the Year Ended November 30, 1999

CAL. A. FORNIA FASHION CENTER

Balance Sheet

December 31, 1999

Assest

Liabilities and Owner's Equity

(c) and (d) General Journal

Date	Account Titles and Explanation	Ref.	Debit	Credit
(c)	Adjustment Entries			
(d)	Closing Entries			

(d) (Continued) General Journal

	Date	Account Titles and Explanation	Ref.	Debit	Credit	
1						1
2						2
3						3
4						4
5						5
6						6
7						7
8						8
9						9
10						10
11						11
12						12
13						13
14						14
15						15

(e)

CAL. A. FORNIA FASHION CENTER
Post-Closing Trial Balance
November 30, 1999

		Debit	Credit	
1				1
2				2
3				3
4				4
5				5
6				6
7				7
8				8
9				9
10				10
11				11
12				12
13				13
14				14
15				15
16				16
17				17

Name | **Problem 5-4B**

Section

Date | **Al Falfa Department Store**

(a)

AL FALFA DEPARTMENT STORE
Income Statement
For the Year Ended November 30, 1999

(a) (Continued)

AL FALFA DEPARTMENT STORE
Income Statement (Continued)
For the Year Ended December 31, 1999

AL FALFA DEPARTMENT STORE
Owner's Equity Statement
For the Year Ended December 31, 1999

(b) General Journal

Date	Account Titles and Explanation	Ref.	Debit	Credit
	Adjustment Entries			

Name **Problem 5-4B Continued**

Section

Date **Al Falfa Department Store**

(a) (Continued)

AL FALFA DEPARTMENT STORE
Balance Sheet
December 31, 1999

Assets

Liabilities and Owner's Equity

Name | **Problem 5-4B Concluded**

Section

Date | **Al Falfa Department Store**

(c) General Journal

Date	Account Titles and Explanation	Ref.	Debit	Credit
	Closing Entries			

Name **Problem 5-5B**

Section

Date **B. J.'s Tennis Shop**

(a) General Journal J1

Date	Account Titles and Explanation	Ref.	Debit	Credit

Name

Section

Date

Problem 5-5B Continued

B. J.'s Tennis Shop

(a) (Continued) General Journal

	Date	Account Titles and Explanation	Ref.	Debit	Credit	
1						1
2						2
3						3
4						4
5						5
6						6
7						7
8						8
9						9
10						10
11						11
12						12
13						13
14						14

(b)

Cash No. 101

Date	Explanation	Ref.	Debit	Credit	Balance

Accounts Receivable No. 112

Date	Explanation	Ref.	Debit	Credit	Balance

Name | **Problem 5-5B Continued**

Section

Date | **B. J.'s Tennis Shop**

(b) (Continued)

Merchandise Inventory — No. 120

Date	Explanation	Ref.	Debit	Credit	Balance

Accounts Payable — No. 201

Date	Explanation	Ref.	Debit	Credit	Balance

B. J. Evans, Capital — No. 301

Date	Explanation	Ref.	Debit	Credit	Balance

Sales — No. 401

Date	Explanation	Ref.	Debit	Credit	Balance

Sales Returns and Allowances — No. 412

Date	Explanation	Ref.	Debit	Credit	Balance

(b) (Continued)

Cost of Goods Sold No. 505

Date	Explanation	Ref.	Debit	Credit	Balance

(c)

B. J.'S TENNIS SHOP
Trial Balance
April 30, 1999

		Debit	Credit	
1				1
2				2
3				3
4				4
5				5
6				6
7				7
8				8
9				9
10				10
11				11
12				12
13				13
14				14

Name

Section

Date

(a) (1) Percentage change in sales —

1996:

1997:

(2) Percentage change in net income —

1996:

1997:

(b) Gross profit rate —

1995:

1996:

1997:

(c) Percentage of net income to sales —

1995:

1996:

1997:

Name

Section

Date

Chapter 5 Comparative Analysis Problem

Kellogg vs. General Mills

(a)	Kellogg	General Mills
(1) 1997 Gross profit		
(2) 1997 Gross profit rate		
(3) 1997 Operating income		
(4) Percentage change in operating income, 1990 to 1997		

(b)

Name

Section

Date

(a)

(b)

(c)

Name

Section

Date

Chapter 5 Group Decision Case

Fedco Department Store

(a) (1)

FEDCO DEPARTMENT STORE

Income Statement

For the Month Ended December 31, 1999

(2)

FEDCO DEPARTMENT STORE

Income Statement

For the Month Ended December 31, 1999

Section

Date

(b)

(c)

FEDCO DEPARTMENT STORE

Income Statement

For the Year Ended December 31, 1999

REAL-WORLD FOCUS A. L. Laboratories

(a)

(b)

(c)

ETHICS CASE Yorkshire Stores

(a)

(b)

Name

Section

Date

(c)

Name

Section

Date

Date	Explanation	Ref.	Debit	Credit	Balance

Date	Explanation	Ref.	Debit	Credit	Balance

Date	Explanation	Ref.	Debit	Credit	Balance

Date	Explanation	Ref.	Debit	Credit	Balance

Name

Section

Date

Name

Section

Date

Name

Section

Date

Exercises 6-1 to 6-2

#1 (a)

(b)

(c)

(d)

#2

Name

Section

Date

Exercise 6-3

Cremer Company

(a) and (b)

General Ledger

Accounts Receivable

Date	Explanation	Ref.	Debit	Credit	Balance

Accounts Receivable Subsidiary Ledger

Alou

Date	Explanation	Ref.	Debit	Credit	Balance

Farr

Date	Explanation	Ref.	Debit	Credit	Balance

George

Date	Explanation	Ref.	Debit	Credit	Balance

Keaton

Date	Explanation	Ref.	Debit	Credit	Balance

Skiles

Date	Explanation	Ref.	Debit	Credit	Balance

Name

Section

Date

#3 (c)

CREMER COMPANY
Schedule of Customers
As of September 30, 1999

1			1
2			2
3			3
4			4
5			5
6			6
7			7
8			8
9			9
10			10
11			11
12			12

#4

HARRIS COMPANY
Sales Journal

S1

Date	Account Debited	Invoice No.	Ref.	Accounts Receiv. Dr. Sales Cr.	COGS Dr. Merchan. Inventory Cr.

HARRIS COMPANY
Purchases Journal

P1

Date	Account Credited	Terms	Ref.	Merchandise Inventory (Dr.) Acc. Pay. (Cr.)

Name
Section
Date

#5

BRIGGS CO.
Cash Receipts Journal
CR1

Date	Account Credited	Ref.	Cash Dr.	Sales Discounts Dr.	Accounts Receivable Cr.	Sales Cr.	Other Accounts Cr.	COGS Dr. Inventory Cr.

BRIGGS CO.
Cash Payments Journal
CP1

Date	Account Debited	Ref.	Other Accounts Dr.	Accounts Payable Dr.	Cash Cr.

#6

	(a) Journal	(b) Journal Columns	
1			1
2			2
3			3
4			4
5			5
6			6
7			7
8			8
9			9
10			10
11			11
12			12
13			13
14			14
15			15

Name

Section

Date

Exercise 6-7

Warner Company

(a)

(b)

Name

Section

Date

#8

#9 (a)

(b)

Name

Section

Date

#10

MOYER COMPANY

(a) Purchases Journal

P1

Date	Account Credited	Terms	Ref.	Merchandise Inventory (Dr.) Acc. Pay. (Cr.)

(b) General Journal

	Date	Account Titles and Explanation	Ref.	Debit	Credit	
1						1
2						2
3						3
4						4
5						5
6						6
7						7
8						8
9						9
10						10
11						11
12						12
13						13
14						14
15						15

#11

1			1
2			2
3			3
4			4
5			5
6			6

Name | **Problem 6-1A**

Section

Date | **Koslo Company**

(a)

KOSLO COMPANY

Cash Receipts Journal

CR1

Date	Account Credited	Ref.	Cash Dr.	Sales Discounts Dr.	Accounts Receivable Cr.	Sales Cr.	Other Accounts Cr.	COGS Dr. Inventory Cr.

(b)

General Ledger

Accounts Receivable

No.112

Date	Explanation	Ref.	Debit	Credit	Balance

(b) (Continued)

Accounts Receivable Subsidiary Ledger

Ben & Son

Date	Explanation	Ref.	Debit	Credit	Balance

Ellis Co.

Date	Explanation	Ref.	Debit	Credit	Balance

Gant Bros.

Date	Explanation	Ref.	Debit	Credit	Balance

Meija Co.

Date	Explanation	Ref.	Debit	Credit	Balance

(c)

Accounts receivable balance:

Sum of subsidiary accounts:

Name Problem 6-2A

Section

Date Cline Company

CLINE COMPANY

(a) Cash Payments Journal CP1

Date	Ck. No.	Account Debited	Ref.	Other Accounts Dr.	Accounts Payable Dr.	Merchan. Inventory Cr.	Cash Cr.

(b) *General Ledger*

Accounts Payable No. 201

Date	Explanation	Ref.	Debit	Credit	Balance

Name

Section

Date

Problem 6-2A Concluded

Cline Company

(b) (Continued)

Accounts Payable Subsidiary Ledger

S. Haley & Co.

Date	Explanation	Ref.	Debit	Credit	Balance

C. King

Date	Explanation	Ref.	Debit	Credit	Balance

W. Ortega

Date	Explanation	Ref.	Debit	Credit	Balance

Welch Bros.

Date	Explanation	Ref.	Debit	Credit	Balance

(c)

1	Accounts payable balance:
2	
3	
4	Sum of subsidiary accounts:
5	
6	
7	
8	
9	
10	

Name **Problem 6-3A**

Section

Date **Pagnozzi Company**

PAGNOZZI COMPANY
Purchases Journal

(a) P1

Date	Account Credited (Debited)	Terms	Ref.	Other Accounts Dr.	Merchan. Inventory Dr.	Accounts Payable Cr.

PAGNOZZI COMPANY
Sales Journal

S1

Date	Account Debited	Invoice No.	Ref.	Accounts Receiv. Dr. Sales Cr.	COGS Dr. Merchandise Inventory Cr.

(a) (Continued)

General Journal

	Date	Account Titles and Explanation	Ref.	Debit	Credit	
1						1
2						2
3						3
4						4
5						5
6						6
7						7
8						8
9						9
10						10
11						11
12						12
13						13
14						14
15						15
16						16
17						17
18						18

(b)

General Ledger

Accounts Receivable — No. 112

Date	Explanation	Ref.	Debit	Credit	Balance

Merchandise Inventory — No. 120

Date	Explanation	Ref.	Debit	Credit	Balance

(b) (Continued)

Supplies No. 126

Date	Explanation	Ref.	Debit	Credit	Balance

Equipment No. 157

Date	Explanation	Ref.	Debit	Credit	Balance

Accounts Payable No. 201

Date	Explanation	Ref.	Debit	Credit	Balance

Sales No. 401

Date	Explanation	Ref.	Debit	Credit	Balance

Sales Returns and Allowances No. 412

Date	Explanation	Ref.	Debit	Credit	Balance

Name
Section
Date

Problem 6-3A Continued

Pagnozzi Company

(b) (Continued)

Cost of Goods Sold — No. 505

Date	Explanation	Ref.	Debit	Credit	Balance

Advertising Expense — No. 610

Date	Explanation	Ref.	Debit	Credit	Balance

Accounts Receivable Subsidiary Ledger

Potts Company

Date	Explanation	Ref.	Debit	Credit	Balance

Hogan Bros.

Date	Explanation	Ref.	Debit	Credit	Balance

Nance Company

Date	Explanation	Ref.	Debit	Credit	Balance

Name | **Problem 6-3A Continued**

Section

Date | **Pagnozzi Company**

(b) (Continued) *Accounts Payable Subsidiary Ledger*

Abel Freight

Date	Explanation	Ref.	Debit	Credit	Balance

Vena Company

Date	Explanation	Ref.	Debit	Credit	Balance

Eaton Supply

Date	Explanation	Ref.	Debit	Credit	Balance

Gore Company

Date	Explanation	Ref.	Debit	Credit	Balance

Deleon Company

Date	Explanation	Ref.	Debit	Credit	Balance

Beck Advertising

Date	Explanation	Ref.	Debit	Credit	Balance

Name

Section

Date

Problem 6-3A Concluded

Pagnozzi Company

(c)

Accounts receivable balance:

Sum of subsidiary accounts:

Accounts payable balance:

Sum of subsidiary accounts:

Name | **Problem 6-4A**
Section
Date | **Santos Company**

(a), (b) and (c)

SANTOS COMPANY
Sales Journal
S1

Date	Account Debited	Invoice No.	Ref.	Accounts Receiv. Dr. Sales Cr.	COGS Dr. Merchan. Inventory Cr.

SANTOS COMPANY
Purchases Journal
P1

Date	Account Credited	Terms	Ref.	Merchandise Inventory (Dr.) Acc. Pay. (Cr.)

General Journal
G1

	Date	Account Titles and Explanation	Ref.	Debit	Credit	
1						1
2						2
3						3
4						4
5						5
6						6
7						7
8						8

(a), (b), and (c) (Continued)

SANTOS COMPANY
Cash Receipts Journal
CR1

Date	Account Credited	Ref.	Cash Dr.	Sales Discounts Dr.	Accounts Receivable Cr.	Sales Cr.	Other Accounts Cr.	COGS Dr. Inventory Cr.

SANTOS COMPANY
Cash Payments Journal
CP1

Date	Account Debited	Ref.	Other Accounts Dr.	Accounts Payable Dr.	Merchan. Inventory Cr.	Cash Cr.

Name **Problem 6-5A**

Section

Date **Tino Co.**

(a), (d) and (g)

General Ledger

Cash No. 101

Date	Explanation	Ref.	Debit	Credit	Balance

Accounts Receivable No. 112

Date	Explanation	Ref.	Debit	Credit	Balance

Merchandise Inventory No. 120

Date	Explanation	Ref.	Debit	Credit	Balance

Supplies No. 126

Date	Explanation	Ref.	Debit	Credit	Balance

Equipment No. 157

Date	Explanation	Ref.	Debit	Credit	Balance

Accumulated Depreciation — Equipment No. 158

Date	Explanation	Ref.	Debit	Credit	Balance

(a), (d) and (g) (Continued)

Accounts Payable — No. 201

Date	Explanation	Ref.	Debit	Credit	Balance

J. Tino, Capital — No. 301

Date	Explanation	Ref.	Debit	Credit	Balance

J. Tino, Drawing — No. 306

Date	Explanation	Ref.	Debit	Credit	Balance

Sales — No. 401

Date	Explanation	Ref.	Debit	Credit	Balance

Sales Discounts — No. 414

Date	Explanation	Ref.	Debit	Credit	Balance

Cost of Goods Sold — No. 505

Date	Explanation	Ref.	Debit	Credit	Balance

(a), (d) and (g) (Continued)

Supplies Expense No. 631

Date	Explanation	Ref.	Debit	Credit	Balance

Depreciation Expense No. 711

Date	Explanation	Ref.	Debit	Credit	Balance

(b)

TINO CO.
Purchases Journal P1

Date	Account Credited	Terms	Ref.	Merchandise Inventory (Dr.) Acc. Pay. (Cr.)

TINO CO.
Cash Payments Journal CP1

Date	Account Debited	Ref.	Other Accounts Dr.	Accounts Payable Dr.	Merchan. Inventory Cr.	Cash Cr.

Name | **Problem 6-5A Continued**
Section
Date | **Tino Co.**

(c)

Accounts Receivable Subsidiary Ledger

D. Alco

Date	Explanation	Ref.	Debit	Credit	Balance

D. Casey

Date	Explanation	Ref.	Debit	Credit	Balance

P. Barber

Date	Explanation	Ref.	Debit	Credit	Balance

K. Dennis

Date	Explanation	Ref.	Debit	Credit	Balance

Accounts Payable Subsidiary Ledger

G. Azar

Date	Explanation	Ref.	Debit	Credit	Balance

J. Carson

Date	Explanation	Ref.	Debit	Credit	Balance

K. Cooper

Date	Explanation	Ref.	Debit	Credit	Balance

(c) (Continued)

M. Kim

Date	Explanation	Ref.	Debit	Credit	Balance

(e)

TINO CO.
Trial Balance
February 28, 1999

		Debit	Credit	
1	Cash			1
2	Accounts Receivable			2
3	Merchandise Inventory			3
4	Supplies			4
5	Equipment			5
6	Accounts Payable			6
7	J. Tino, Capital			7
8	J. Tino, Drawing			8
9	Sales			9
10	Sales Discounts			10
11	Cost of Goods Sold			11
12				12
13				13

(f)

1	Accounts receivable control account:			1
2				2
3	Accounts receivable subsidiary accounts:			3
4				4
5				5
6				6
7				7
8	Accounts payable control account:			8
9				9
10	Accounts payable subsidiary accounts:			10
11				11
12				12
13				13

(g) General Journal G1

	Date	Account Titles and Explanation	Ref.	Debit	Credit	
1						1
2						2
3						3
4						4
5						5
6						6
7						7
8						8
9						9
10						10

(h)

TINO CO.
Adjusted Trial Balance
February 28, 1999

		Debit	Credit	
1	Cash			1
2	Accounts Receivable			2
3	Merchandise Inventory			3
4	Supplies			4
5	Equipment			5
6	Accumulated Depreciation—Equipment			6
7	Accounts Payable			7
8	J. Tino, Capital			8
9	J. Tino, Drawing			9
10	Sales			10
11	Sales Discounts			11
12	Cost of Goods Sold			12
13	Supplies Expense			13
14	Depreciation Expense			14
15				15
16				16
17				17
18				18
19				19
20				20

Name | **Problem 6-6A**

Section

Date | **Gonzalez Co.**

(b)

GONZALEZ CO.
Sales Journal

S1

Date	Account Debited	Invoice No.	Ref.	Accounts Receiv. Dr. Sales Cr.	COGS Dr. Merchan. Inventory Cr.

GONZALEZ CO.
Purchases Journal

P1

Date	Account Credited	Terms	Ref.	Merchandise Inventory Dr. Acc. Pay. Cr.

General Journal

G1

	Date	Account Titles and Explanation	Ref.	Debit	Credit	
1						1
2						2
3						3
4						4
5						5
6						6
7						7
8						8
9						9
10						10
11						11
12						12
13						13
14						14
15						15

(b) (Continued)

GONZALEZ CO.
Cash Receipts Journal

CR1

Date	Account Credited	Ref.	Cash Dr.	Sales Discounts Dr.	Accounts Receivable Cr.	Sales Cr.	Other Accounts Cr.	COGS Dr. Inventory Cr.

GONZALEZ CO.
Cash Payments Journal

CP1

Date	Account Debited	Ref.	Other Accounts Dr.	Accounts Payable Dr.	Merchan. Inventory Cr.	Cash Cr.

(a) and (c)

General Ledger

Cash

No. 101

Date	Explanation	Ref.	Debit	Credit	Balance

Name

Section

Date

Problem 6-6A Continued

Gonzalez Company

(a) and (c)

Accounts Receivable — No. 112

Date	Explanation	Ref.	Debit	Credit	Balance

Notes Receivable — No. 115

Date	Explanation	Ref.	Debit	Credit	Balance

Merchandise Inventory — No. 120

Date	Explanation	Ref.	Debit	Credit	Balance

Equipment — No. 157

Date	Explanation	Ref.	Debit	Credit	Balance

Accumulated Depreciation — Equipment — No. 158

Date	Explanation	Ref.	Debit	Credit	Balance

Notes Payable — No. 200

Date	Explanation	Ref.	Debit	Credit	Balance

Name | **Problem 6-6A Continued**
Section
Date | **Gonzalez Co.**

(a) and (c) (Continued)

Accounts Payable — No. 201

Date	Explanation	Ref.	Debit	Credit	Balance

L. Gonzalez, Capital — No. 301

Date	Explanation	Ref.	Debit	Credit	Balance

Sales — No. 401

Date	Explanation	Ref.	Debit	Credit	Balance

Sales Returns and Allowances — No. 412

Date	Explanation	Ref.	Debit	Credit	Balance

Sales Discounts — No. 414

Date	Explanation	Ref.	Debit	Credit	Balance

Cost of Goods Sold — No. 505

Date	Explanation	Ref.	Debit	Credit	Balance

(a) and (c) (Continued)

Sales Salaries Expense No. 627

Date	Explanation	Ref.	Debit	Credit	Balance

Office Salaries Expense No. 727

Date	Explanation	Ref.	Debit	Credit	Balance

Rent Expense No. 729

Date	Explanation	Ref.	Debit	Credit	Balance

Accounts Receivable Subsidiary Ledger

P. Naab

Date	Explanation	Ref.	Debit	Credit	Balance

K. Hoyt

Date	Explanation	Ref.	Debit	Credit	Balance

A. Dietz

Date	Explanation	Ref.	Debit	Credit	Balance

Name

Section

Date

Problem 6-6A Continued

Gonzalez Co.

(a) and (c) (Continued)

C. Hernandez

Date	Explanation	Ref.	Debit	Credit	Balance

Accounts Payable Subsidiary Ledger

B. Masoni

Date	Explanation	Ref.	Debit	Credit	Balance

D. Kraft

Date	Explanation	Ref.	Debit	Credit	Balance

W. Henrie

Date	Explanation	Ref.	Debit	Credit	Balance

J. Fanning

Date	Explanation	Ref.	Debit	Credit	Balance

D. Greer

Date	Explanation	Ref.	Debit	Credit	Balance

Name Problem 6-6A Concluded

Section

Date Gonzalez Co.

(d)

GONZALEZ CO.
Trial Balance
January 31, 1999

		Debit	Credit	
1	Cash			1
2	Accounts Receivable			2
3	Notes Receivable			3
4	Merchandise Inventory			4
5	Equipment			5
6	Accumulated Depreciation—Equipment			6
7	Notes Payable			7
8	Accounts Payable			8
9	L. Gonzalez, Capital			9
10	Sales			10
11	Sales Returns and Allowances			11
12	Sales Discounts			12
13	Cost of Goods Sold			13
14	Sales Salaries Expense			14
15	Office Salaries Expense			15
16	Rent Expense			16
17				17
18				18
19				19

(e)

1	Accounts receivable subsidiary ledger:			1
2				2
3				3
4				4
5				5
6				6
7	Accounts receivable control:			7
8				8
9	Accounts payable subsidiary ledger:			9
10				10
11				11
12				12
13				13
14				14
15	Accounts payable control:			15
16				16

Name | **Problem 6-1B**
Section
Date | **Morrow Company**

(a)

MORROW COMPANY
Cash Receipts Journal

CR1

Date	Account Credited	Ref.	Cash Dr.	Sales Discounts Dr.	Accounts Receivable Cr.	Sales Cr.	Other Accounts Cr.	COGS Dr. Inventory Cr.

(b)

General Ledger
Accounts Receivable

No.112

Date	Explanation	Ref.	Debit	Credit	Balance

(b) (Continued) *Accounts Receivable Subsidiary Ledger*

Horner

Date	Explanation	Ref.	Debit	Credit	Balance

Kole

Date	Explanation	Ref.	Debit	Credit	Balance

Micci Co.

Date	Explanation	Ref.	Debit	Credit	Balance

Starr

Date	Explanation	Ref.	Debit	Credit	Balance

(c)

1	Accounts receivable balance:	1
2		2
3		3
4	Sum of subsidiary accounts:	4
5		5
6		6
7		7
8		8
9		9
10		10

Name — Problem 6-2B

Section

Date — Norton Company

NORTON COMPANY

(a) Cash Payments Journal — CP1

Date	Ck. No.	Account Debited	Ref.	Other Accounts Dr.	Accounts Payable Dr.	Merchan. Inventory Cr.	Cash Cr.

(b) *General Ledger*

Accounts Payable — No. 201

Date	Explanation	Ref.	Debit	Credit	Balance

(b) (Continued)

Accounts Payable Subsidiary Ledger

Heston Company

Date	Explanation	Ref.	Debit	Credit	Balance

Menke & Sons

Date	Explanation	Ref.	Debit	Credit	Balance

Paige Company

Date	Explanation	Ref.	Debit	Credit	Balance

Ogle

Date	Explanation	Ref.	Debit	Credit	Balance

(c)

1	Accounts payable balance:	1
2		2
3		3
4	Sum of subsidiary accounts:	4
5		5
6		6
7		7
8		8
9		9
10		10

Name **Problem 6-3B**

Section

Date **Cruz Company**

(a)

CRUZ COMPANY

Purchases Journal

P1

Date	Account Credited (Debited)	Terms	Ref.	Other Accounts Dr.	Merchan. Inventory Dr.	Accounts Payable Cr.

CRUZ COMPANY

Sales Journal

S1

Date	Account Debited	Invoice No.	Ref.	Accounts Receiv. Dr. Sales Cr.	COGS Dr. Merchandise Inventory Cr.

Name **Problem 6-3B Continued**

Section

Date **Cruz Company**

(a) (Continued) General Journal G1

Date	Account Titles and Explanation	Ref.	Debit	Credit

(b)

General Ledger

Accounts Receivable No. 112

Date	Explanation	Ref.	Debit	Credit	Balance

Merchandise Inventory No. 120

Date	Explanation	Ref.	Debit	Credit	Balance

Name | Problem 6-3B Continued
Section
Date | Cruz Company

(b) (Continued)

Supplies — No. 126

Date	Explanation	Ref.	Debit	Credit	Balance

Equipment — No. 157

Date	Explanation	Ref.	Debit	Credit	Balance

Accounts Payable — No. 201

Date	Explanation	Ref.	Debit	Credit	Balance

Sales — No. 401

Date	Explanation	Ref.	Debit	Credit	Balance

Sales Returns and Allowances — No. 412

Date	Explanation	Ref.	Debit	Credit	Balance

Cost of Goods Sold — No. 505

Date	Explanation	Ref.	Debit	Credit	Balance

Advertising Expense — No. 610

Date	Explanation	Ref.	Debit	Credit	Balance

Name | **Problem 6-3B Continued**

Section

Date | **Cruz Company**

(b) (Continued)

Accounts Receivable Subsidiary Ledger

Flood Bros.

Date	Explanation	Ref.	Debit	Credit	Balance

Laird Co.

Date	Explanation	Ref.	Debit	Credit	Balance

Marquez Company

Date	Explanation	Ref.	Debit	Credit	Balance

Resch Company

Date	Explanation	Ref.	Debit	Credit	Balance

Accounts Payable Subsidiary Ledger

Beyer Supply

Date	Explanation	Ref.	Debit	Credit	Balance

Carlin Shipping

Date	Explanation	Ref.	Debit	Credit	Balance

Name **Problem 6-3B Continued**

Section

Date **Cruz Company**

(b) (Continued)

DeVito Company

Date	Explanation	Ref.	Debit	Credit	Balance

Granger Company

Date	Explanation	Ref.	Debit	Credit	Balance

Meyer's Advertisements

Date	Explanation	Ref.	Debit	Credit	Balance

Reeble Company

Date	Explanation	Ref.	Debit	Credit	Balance

Name

Section

Date

Cruz Company

(c)

Accounts receivable balance:

Sum of subsidiary accounts:

Accounts payable balance:

Sum of subsidiary accounts:

Name | **Problem 6-4B**

Section

Date | **Shell Company**

(a), (b), and (c)

SHELL COMPANY
Sales Journal
S1

Date	Account Debited	Invoice No.	Ref.	Accounts Receiv. Dr. Sales Cr.	COGS Dr. Merchandise Inventory Cr.

SHELL COMPANY
Purchases Journal
P1

Date	Account Credited	Terms	Ref.	Merchandise Inventory (Dr.) Acc. Pay. (Cr.)

General Journal
G1

1			1
2			2
3			3
4			4
5			5
6			6
7			7
8			8
9			9

Name **Problem 6-4B Concluded**

Section

Date **Shell Company**

(a), (b), and (c) (Continued)

SHELL COMPANY
Cash Receipts Journal

CR1

Date	Account Credited	Ref.	Cash Dr.	Sales Discounts Dr.	Accounts Receivable Cr.	Sales Cr.	Other Accounts Cr.	COGS Dr. Inventory Cr.

SHELL COMPANY
Cash Payments Journal

CP1

Date	Account Debited	Ref.	Other Accounts Dr.	Accounts Payable Dr.	Merchan. Inventory Cr.	Cash Cr.

Name	Problem 6-5B
Section	
Date	Weber Co.

(a), (d) and (g)

General Ledger

Cash — No. 101

Date	Explanation	Ref.	Debit	Credit	Balance

Accounts Receivable — No. 112

Date	Explanation	Ref.	Debit	Credit	Balance

Merchandise Inventory — No. 120

Date	Explanation	Ref.	Debit	Credit	Balance

Store Supplies — No. 127

Date	Explanation	Ref.	Debit	Credit	Balance

Prepaid Rent — No. 131

Date	Explanation	Ref.	Debit	Credit	Balance

Accounts Payable — No. 201

Date	Explanation	Ref.	Debit	Credit	Balance

Name | **Problem 6-5B Continued**

Section

Date | **Weber Co.**

(a), (d) and (g) (Continued)

Weber, Capital — No. 301

Date	Explanation	Ref.	Debit	Credit	Balance

Weber, Drawing — No. 306

Date	Explanation	Ref.	Debit	Credit	Balance

Sales — No. 401

Date	Explanation	Ref.	Debit	Credit	Balance

Sales Returns and Allowances — No. 412

Date	Explanation	Ref.	Debit	Credit	Balance

Sales Discounts — No. 414

Date	Explanation	Ref.	Debit	Credit	Balance

Cost of Goods Sold — No. 505

Date	Explanation	Ref.	Debit	Credit	Balance

Supplies Expense — No. 631

Date	Explanation	Ref.	Debit	Credit	Balance

Name | | **Problem 6-5B Continued**
Section
Date | | **Weber Co.**

(a), (d) and (g) (Continued)

Rent Expense — No. 729

Date	Explanation	Ref.	Debit	Credit	Balance

(b)

WEBER CO.
Cash Receipts Journal — CR1

Date	Account Credited	Ref.	Cash Dr.	Sales Discounts Dr.	Accounts Receivable Cr.	Sales Cr.	Other Accounts Cr.	COGS Dr. Inventory Cr.

WEBER CO.
Sales Journal — S1

Date	Account Debited	Invoice No.	Ref.	Accounts Receiv. Dr. Sales Cr.	COGS Dr. Merchandise Inventory Cr.

Name

Section

Date

Problem 6-5B Continued

Weber Co.

(c) *Accounts Payable Subsidiary Ledger*

C. Hunt

Date	Explanation	Ref.	Debit	Credit	Balance

S. Faur

Date	Explanation	Ref.	Debit	Credit	Balance

R. Jenks

Date	Explanation	Ref.	Debit	Credit	Balance

P. Coley

Date	Explanation	Ref.	Debit	Credit	Balance

B. Goltra

Date	Explanation	Ref.	Debit	Credit	Balance

(c) (Continued) *Accounts Receivable Subsidiary Ledger*

Lentz Co.

Date	Explanation	Ref.	Debit	Credit	Balance

A. Kear

Date	Explanation	Ref.	Debit	Credit	Balance

G. Linton

Date	Explanation	Ref.	Debit	Credit	Balance

J. Wegner

Date	Explanation	Ref.	Debit	Credit	Balance

(e)

WEBER CO.
Trial Balance
July 31, 1999

		Debit	Credit	
1	Cash			1
2	Accounts Receivable			2
3	Merchandise Inventory			3
4	Store Supplies			4
5	Prepaid Rent			5
6	Accounts Payable			6
7	Weber, Capital			7
8	Weber, Drawing			8
9	Sales			9
10	Sales Discounts			10
11	Cost of Goods Sold			11
12				12
13				13
14				14
15				15

(f)

1				1
2	Accounts receivable control account:			2
3				3
4	Accounts receivable subsidiary accounts:			4
5				5
6				6
7				7
8				8
9	Accounts payable control account:			9
10				10
11	Accounts payable subsidiary accounts:			11
12				12
13				13
14				14
15				15

Name
Section
Date

Problem 6-5B Concluded

Weber Co.

(b) and (g) General Journal G1

	Date	Account Titles and Explanation	Ref.	Debit	Credit	
1						1
2						2
3						3
4						4
5						5
6						6
7						7
8						8
9						9
10						10
11						11
12						12
13						13
14						14
15						15

(h)

WEBER CO.
Adjusted Trial Balance
July 31, 1999

		Debit	Credit	
1	Cash			1
2	Accounts Receivable			2
3	Merchandise Inventory			3
4	Store Supplies			4
5	Prepaid Rent			5
6	Accounts Payable			6
7	Weber, Capital			7
8	Weber, Drawing			8
9	Sales			9
10	Sales Discounts			10
11	Cost of Goods Sold			11
12	Supplies Expense			12
13	Rent Expense			13
14				14
15				15

Name
Section
Date

Stone Co. (Mini Practice Set)

(a)

STONE CO.
Sales Journal

S1

Date	Account Debited	Invoice No.	Ref.	Accounts Receiv. Dr. Sales Cr.	COGS Dr. Merchan. Inventory Cr.

STONE CO.
Purchases Journal

P1

Date	Account Credited	Terms	Ref.	Merchandise Inventory Dr. Acc. Pay. Cr.

(a) (Continued)

STONE CO.
Cash Receipts Journal

CR1

Date	Account Credited	Ref.	Cash Dr.	Sales Discounts Dr.	Accounts Receivable Cr.	Sales Cr.	Other Accounts Cr.	COGS Dr. Inventory Cr.

(a) (Continued)

STONE CO.
Cash Payments Journal CR1

Date	Account Debited	Ref.	Other Accounts Dr.	Accounts Payable Dr.	Office Supplies Dr.	Merchan. Inventory Cr.	Cash Cr.

(a) (Continued) General Journal G1

	Date	Account Titles and Explanation	Ref.	Debit	Credit	
1						1
2						2
3						3
4						4
5						5
6						6
7						7
8						8
9						9
10						10
11						11
12						12
13						13
14						14
15						15
16						16
17						17
18						18
19						19
20						20
21						21
22						22
23						23
24						24
25						25
26						26
27						27
28						28
29						29
30						30
31						31
32						32
33						33
34						34
35						35
36						36
37						37
38						38
39						39
40						40

(b) and (e)

General Ledger

Cash No. 101

Date	Explanation	Ref.	Debit	Credit	Balance
Jan. 1	Balance	✓			35750

Accounts Receivable No. 112

Date	Explanation	Ref.	Debit	Credit	Balance
Jan. 1	Balance	✓			13000

Notes Receivable No. 115

Date	Explanation	Ref.	Debit	Credit	Balance
Jan. 1	Balance	✓			39000

Merchandise Inventory No. 120

Date	Explanation	Ref.	Debit	Credit	Balance
Jan. 1	Balance	✓			18000

Office Supplies No. 125

Date	Explanation	Ref.	Debit	Credit	Balance
Jan. 1	Balance	✓			1000

(b) and (e) (Continued)

Prepaid Insurance No. 130

Date	Explanation	Ref.	Debit	Credit	Balance
Jan. 1	Balance	✓			2000

Equipment No. 157

Date	Explanation	Ref.	Debit	Credit	Balance
Jan. 1	Balance	✓			6450

Accumulated Depreciation — Equipment No. 158

Date	Explanation	Ref.	Debit	Credit	Balance
Jan. 1	Balance	✓			1500

Notes Payable No. 200

Date	Explanation	Ref.	Debit	Credit	Balance

Accounts Payable No. 201

Date	Explanation	Ref.	Debit	Credit	Balance
Jan. 1	Balance	✓			35000

Interest Payable No. 230

Date	Explanation	Ref.	Debit	Credit	Balance

(b) and (e) (Continued)

M. Stone, Capital — No. 301

Date	Explanation	Ref.	Debit	Credit	Balance
Jan. 1	Balance	✓			78700

M. Stone, Drawing — No. 306

Date	Explanation	Ref.	Debit	Credit	Balance

Income Summary — No. 350

Date	Explanation	Ref.	Debit	Credit	Balance

Sales — No. 401

Date	Explanation	Ref.	Debit	Credit	Balance

Sales Returns and Allowances — No. 412

Date	Explanation	Ref.	Debit	Credit	Balance

(b) and (e) (Continued)

Sales Discounts No. 414

Date	Explanation	Ref.	Debit	Credit	Balance

Interest Revenue No. 430

Date	Explanation	Ref.	Debit	Credit	Balance

Cost of Goods Sold No. 505

Date	Explanation	Ref.	Debit	Credit	Balance

Sales Salaries Expense No. 627

Date	Explanation	Ref.	Debit	Credit	Balance

(b) and (e) (Continued)

Depreciation Expense No. 711

Date	Explanation	Ref.	Debit	Credit	Balance

Interest Expense No. 718

Date	Explanation	Ref.	Debit	Credit	Balance

Insurance Expense No. 722

Date	Explanation	Ref.	Debit	Credit	Balance

Office Salaries Expense No. 727

Date	Explanation	Ref.	Debit	Credit	Balance

Office Supplies Expense No. 728

Date	Explanation	Ref.	Debit	Credit	Balance

Rent Expense No. 729

Date	Explanation	Ref.	Debit	Credit	Balance

(b) and (e) (Continued)

Accounts Receivable Subsidiary Ledger

R. Dansig

Date	Explanation	Ref.	Debit	Credit	Balance
Jan. 1	Balance	✓			1500

J. Eaton

Date	Explanation	Ref.	Debit	Credit	Balance

B. Jaggar

Date	Explanation	Ref.	Debit	Credit	Balance
Jan. 1	Balance	✓			7500

S. Lowell

Date	Explanation	Ref.	Debit	Credit	Balance
Jan. 1	Balance	✓			4000

B. Sargent

Date	Explanation	Ref.	Debit	Credit	Balance

(b) and (e) (Continued)

Accounts Payable Subsidiary Ledger

D. Landell

Date	Explanation	Ref.	Debit	Credit	Balance

S. Lee

Date	Explanation	Ref.	Debit	Credit	Balance
Jan. 1	Balance	✓			9000

R. Mannon

Date	Explanation	Ref.	Debit	Credit	Balance
Jan. 1	Balance	✓			15000

D. Nordin

Date	Explanation	Ref.	Debit	Credit	Balance
Jan. 1	Balance	✓			11000

S. Walden

Date	Explanation	Ref.	Debit	Credit	Balance

Additional working papers for this practice set are at the back of this book

(d)

STONE CO.
Income Statement
For the Month Ended January 31, 1999

(d) (Continued)

STONE CO.
Owner's Equity Statement
For the Month Ended January 31, 1999

STONE CO.
Balance Sheet
January 31, 1999

Assets

Liabilities and Owner's Equity

Name

Section

Date

(e) General Journal G1

Date	Account Titles and Explanation	Ref.	Debit	Credit
	Closing Entries			

Name

Section

Date

(f)

STONE CO.
Post-Closing Trial Balance
January 31, 1999

	Debit	Credit
Cash		
Notes Receivable		
Accounts Receivable		
Merchandise Inventory		
Office Supplies		
Prepaid Insurance		
Equipment		
Accumulated Depreciation—Equipment		
Notes Payable		
Accounts Payable		
Interest Payable		
M. Stone, Capital		

Accounts receivable balance:		
Sum of subsidiary accounts:		
Accounts payable balance:		
Sum of subsidiary accounts:		

Name

Section

Date

(a)

(a) (Continued)

(b)

(c)

Name | **Chapter 6 Real-World Focus**

Section

Date | **Chapter 6 Ethics Case**

REAL-WORLD FOCUS — Alco Standard Corporation

(a)

(b)

ETHICS CASE — Tyler Products Company

Name

Section

Date

(a)

WATERWORL

W

For the Year En

Account Titles	Trial Balance Dr.	Trial Balance Cr.	Adjustm Dr.
Cash	37400		
Supplies	18600		
Prepaid Insurance	31900		
Land	80000		
Equipment	120000		
Accumulated Depreciation		36200	
Accounts Payable		14600	
Unearned Admission Revenue		2700	
Mortgage Payable		50000	
N. Y. Berge, Capital		109700	
N. Y. Berge, Drawing	14000		
Admission Revenue		278500	
Salaries Expense	109000		
Repair Expense	30500		
Advertising Expense	9400		
Utilities Expense	16900		
Property Taxes Expense	18000		
Interest Expense	6000		
Totals	491700	491700	
Insurance Expense			
Supplies Expense			
Interest Payable			
Depreciation Expense			
Property Taxes Payable			
Totals			
Net Income			

AMUSEMENT PARK
rk Sheet
ed September 30, 1999

nts	Adjusted Trial Balance		Income Statement		Balance Sheet	
Cr.	Dr.	Cr.	Dr.	Cr.	Dr.	Cr.

Name

Section

Date

S

W

(c) For the Month

	Account Titles	Trial Balance		Adjustm	
		Dr.	Cr.	Dr.	
1	Cash				
2	Accounts Receivable				
3	Notes Receivable				
4	Merchandise Inventory				
5	Office Supplies				
6	Prepaid Insurance				
7	Equipment				
8	Accumulated Depreciation—Equipment				
9	Notes Payable				
10	Accounts Payable				
11	Interest Payable				
12	M. Stone, Capital				
13	M. Stone, Drawing				
14	Sales				
15	Sales Returns and Allowances				
16	Sales Discounts				
17	Cost of Goods Sold				
18	Sales Salaries Expense				
19	Office Salaries Expense				
20	Rent Expense				
21					
22	Totals				
23					
24	Office Supplies Expense				
25	Insurance Expense				
26	Depreciation Expense				
27	Interest Expense				
28					
29	Totals				
30	Net Income				
31	Totals				
32					
33					
34					
35					
36					
37					
38					
39					
40					

ONE CO.
ork Sheet
nded January 31, 1999

ents	Adjusted Trial Balance		Income Statement		Balance Sheet	
Cr.	Dr.	Cr.	Dr.	Cr.	Dr.	Cr.